Contents

Foreword

The main aim of this series is to focus on different approaches to stress counselling and management. It is intended that the books will link theory and research to the practice of stress counselling and stress management. Leading counselling, clinical, health and occupational psychologists, biologists, counsellors and psychotherapists will report on their work, focusing on individual, group and organizational interventions.

The books will interest both undergraduate and postgraduate students as well as experienced practitioners in the helping professions. In particular, those who work in the fields of counselling, psychology, psychotherapy, sociology and mental and occupational health.

This book, *Stress Management and Counselling*, is the first book in the *Stress Counselling* series. It is hoped that it provides an insight into the type of work leading practitioners and academics are currently undertaking in the fields of stress research, stress management and stress counselling.

Stephen Palmer
Centre for Stress Management, London

Preface

We recently edited a special symposium document entitled *Stress Management and Counselling* for the *British Journal of Guidance and Counselling*. This symposium created a fair amount of interest as it focused on theory, practice, research and methodology, linking the fields of stress management and counselling. One of the objectives of the symposium was to provide trainee and experienced counsellors, psychologists and health professionals with a valuable overview of the subject. In our experience of teaching counsellors, we have found that few have really grasped the biological aspects of stress and its management and therefore we commissioned a paper on this important topic. This paper linked with the article on rational emotive behaviour therapy highlights the psychobiological connection between appraisal and the subsequent physiological response to stress. The symposium included a paper on *A person-centred approach to stress management*, a topic which is rarely written about even though the person-centred approach is one of the major forms of counselling practised in Britain. We have included additional papers in this book to cover topics that were not included in the symposium due to space restrictions. Where necessary, authors have updated the papers.

This book is divided into four sections. Part I is the Introduction, featuring a chapter focusing on professional concerns regarding the training of stress management practitioners and on some of the issues raised by the remaining chapters of this book. Part II explores the Biological Basis of Stress Management in sufficient detail to help counsellors and health professionals explain the physiological aspects of the stress response to their clients. Part III looks at the Theory and Practice of Stress Management and Counselling. This comprises three chapters which examine different therapeutic approaches to stress counselling and stress management, as well as a public health model for dealing with traumatic stress at work. Chapter 7 considers the importance of counselling and stress management training and also argues for more substantive organizational change through stress audits. Part IV examines Stress Management: Research, Issues and Methodology. Essentially this reviews the research and looks at some of the conceptual and methodological issues involved in the study of stress management. In the final chapter we are reminded that:

Stress research is in serious danger of being recognized as yet another short-lived fad unless a more reasoned, measured and critical approach is taken by its most vocal proponents. Without a fuller conceptual grasp of the problems people experience at work and the possible consequences of such problems, the means to alleviate them will remain elusive.

We hope that this book goes some way towards keeping the different problems and issues on both the researcher's and the practitioner's agendas.

Stephen Palmer and Windy Dryden

Acknowledgements

Chapter 1 by Stephen Palmer and Windy Dryden is a revised and expanded version on an article first published in the *British Journal of Guidance & Counselling* **22**:1 (1994), 5–12.

Chapter 2 by Olga Gregson and Terry Looker, Chapter 3 by Peter Clarke, Chapter 5 by Michael Abrams and Albert Ellis, Chapter 6 by David Richards, Chapter 7 by Cary Cooper and Sue Cartwright, and Chapter 11 by Shirley Reynolds and Rob Briner were first published in the *British Journal of Guidance & Counselling* **22**:1 (1994), 13–26, 27–37, 39–50, 51–64, 65–73, and 75–89.

Chapter 4 by Stephen Palmer is a revised and expanded version of an article first published in *Counselling, Journal of the British Association for Counselling* **3**:4 (1992), 220–24, and includes a section from *Counselling for Stress Problems* published by Sage, London, 1995, pp. 4–6.

Chapter 8 by Paul Bennett and Douglas Carroll was first published in the *British Journal of Clinical Psychology* **29**:1 (1990), 1–12.

Chapter 9 by Philip Dewe, Tom Cox and Eamonn Ferguson was first published in *Work and Stress* **7**:1 (1993), 5–15.

Chapter 10 by Michael O'Driscoll and Cary Cooper was first published in the *Journal of Occupational and Organizational Psychology* **67**:4 (1994), 343–54.

The editors and publishers wish to thank the following for permission to reprint copyright material: Careers Research and Advisory Centre for Chapters 1, 2, 3, 5, 6, 7 and 11; Sage Publications and the British Association for Counselling for Chapter 4; the British Psychological Society for Chapters 8 and 10; and Taylor & Francis for Chapter 9.

Every effort has been made to trace all copyright holders, but if any parties have been inadvertently overlooked, we shall be pleased to include an acknowledgement at the next opportunity.

Contributors

Michael Abrams is President of Psychological Health Group, a private non-profit mental health centre, where he uses Rational Emotive Behaviour Therapy with all mental health problems. He has co-authored two books with Albert Ellis, *How to Cope With a Fatal Illness* and *The Art and Science of Rational Eating*.

Paul Bennett currently works as a Consultant Clinical Psychologist with Gwent Psychology Services and has an honorary lectureship with the University of Wales. He obtained his Master's degree in Clinical Psychology at Plymouth University, and his Ph.D. at Birmingham University. He has published over 50 articles in scientific journals and has authored a book on counselling in heart disease. His present research interests include interventions and predictors of outcome in cardiac rehabilitation as well as a wider interest in health promotion and social-cognition models.

Rob B. Briner is a lecturer in Organizational Psychology at Birkbeck College, London. He has degrees from Hull, Durham and Sheffield Universities. He has been involved in research on stress and health for over ten years. Other research interests include goal setting, retirement planning and mood regulation processes.

Douglas Carroll is currently Professor of Applied Psychology in the School of Sport and Exercise Sciences at the University of Birmingham. He gained a B.Sc. in Psychology from the University of Edinburgh and a Ph.D. at the Australian National University. He is author or co-author of five books, including *Health Psychology: Stress, Behaviour and Disease* and (with Catherine Niven) *The Health Psychology of Women*, and some hundred journal articles and book chapters.

Sue Cartwright is a Senior Research Fellow in Organizational Psychology at the Manchester School of Management, University of Manchester Institute of Science and Technology. She is also Director of the Centre for Business Psychology, an applied research/consultancy unit based in the School. She has published widely in the field of occupational stress and has worked with many public and private sector organizations advising on stress intervention strategies.

Peter Clarke is a Senior Lecturer at the Department of Educational Studies, Faculty of Education, Jordanhill Campus, Strathclyde University. In addition, he is a person-centred therapist, a supervisor and a sports psychologist.

Cary L. Cooper is currently Professor of Organizational Psychology of the Manchester School of Management, University of Manchester Institute of Science and Technology. He is the author of over 70 books, has written over 250 scholarly articles for academic journals, and is a frequent contributor to national newspapers. He is currently Editor-in-Chief of the *Journal of Organizational Behavior*, and Co-Editor of *Stress Medicine*.

Tom Cox is Professor of Organizational Psychology at the Department of Psychology, University of Nottingham. He is Director of the Centre for Organizational Health & Development, University of Nottingham. He is Managing Editor of *Work and Stress*.

Philip Dewe is Professor and Head of the Department of Human Resource Management, Faculty of Business, Massey University, Palmerston North, New Zealand. He was for a number of years a Senior Research Officer with the Work Research Unit and has published widely in the area of work stress and coping. He has also been Research Fellow in the Department of Organizational Psychology, Birkbeck College; the Department of Industrial Relations, London School of Economics; and Erasmus University, Rotterdam.

Michael O'Driscoll is Associate Professor and Head of Psychology, University of Waikato, New Zealand. He has published widely in the field of workplace stress and other areas of industrial and organizational psycholgy.

Windy Dryden is Professor of Counselling at Goldsmiths College, University of London. He is a chartered psychologist, a UKCP registered psychotherapist, a BAC accredited counsellor and a Fellow of the British Psychological Society. He has edited or authored over 100 books, and many articles and book chapters.

Albert Ellis is President of the Institute for Rational-Emotive Therapy, New York City. He is founder of Rational Emotive Behaviour Therapy. He is the author of over 50 books, including *Reason and Emotion in Psychotherapy*, revised and updated, published by Carol Publishing Group, New York.

Eamonn Ferguson is a member of the WHO collaborating Centre for Organizational Health & Development and a lecturer in Psychology at the University of Nottingham. His research interests include stress, coping and health, blood donor behaviour, occupational HIV risk perception and hypochondriasis. He has published numerous academic articles and presented many conference papers on these topics.

Olga Gregson graduated from the University of Wales in 1974 with an Honours degree, then specialized in behaviour and visual perception at the Victoria University of Manchester, where she received her doctorate in 1981. From there she joined the Department of Biological Sciences at Manchester Metropolitan University where she is Senior Lecturer in physiology and behaviour.

Professor Terry Looker graduated from London University in 1969 with an Honours degree and received his doctorate in 1972 from Guy's Hospital Medical School. He has been lecturing in the Department of Biological Sciences at Metropolitan University since 1973 and was appointed Head of Department in 1989. He lectures and researches in the areas of cardiovascular physiology, stress and health.

Stephen Palmer is Director of the Centre for Stress Management, London, and an Honorary Visiting Lecturer in Psychology at Goldsmiths College, University of London. He is a chartered psychologist, a UKCP registered psychotherapist and a Fellow of the Royal Society of Health. He edits or co-edits three professional counselling and health education journals and has authored or co-authored eleven books and training manuals.

Shirley Reynolds is Academic Course Organizer for Clinical Psychology at the University of East Anglia. Her research interests span clinical and organizational psychology with particular interests in applications in developing health services. Current research activities include organizational stress interventions, psychotherapy process and outcome and mood regulation processes.

David Richards is the Research and Development Co-ordinator for Leeds Community and Mental Health Services Trust and was previously Counselling Co-ordinator for the Leeds Permanent Building Society. He qualified initially as a psychiatric nurse in Cambridge and then moved on to train as a behavioural psychotherapist in London. Before joining the Leeds he worked as a therapist, researcher and lecturer in Psychotherapy at the Institute of Psychiatry and Maudsley Hospital, London. He has published widely.

PART ONE
Introduction

CHAPTER 1

Stress Management & Counselling: Approaches and Interventions

Stephen Palmer and Windy Dryden

INTRODUCTION

In this and the last decade, the interest in stress management interventions at the individual and organizational level has grown. There has almost been an exponential increase in the publication of research papers in this field of work. However, some researchers believe that the value of stress management interventions still needs to be properly assessed (e.g. Reynolds and Briner, Chapter 11).

In this chapter we will focus on our professional concerns regarding the training of stress management practitioners and on the issues raised by the remaining chapters of this book.

PROFESSIONAL CONCERNS

How can the purchaser of stress management services choose a suitable consultancy that uses an 'accepted' approach? Not only has there been a growing interest in stress, but the number of consultants or 'experts' offering stress management services has also increased in the past decade. The recession has opened up a new market for the training of non-professionals in stress management particularly those who have been made redundant. The advertising of relevant courses in the British national press may reflect this trend. Although we are not necessarily doubting the quality of such courses, we are concerned about whether the layperson can grasp the complexities of stress, stress counselling and stress management interventions over a couple of weekends or by means of a correspondence course. Also, is a course that only teaches a layperson one basic approach such as hypnosis or relaxation sufficient to enable them to help the majority of their potential organizational and individual clients? We very much doubt it. However, an experienced psychologist, counsellor or health professional may find a short course, relevant reading and supervision adequate to undertake stress counselling and stress management interventions.

We have been involved in 'training the trainers' in stress management and counselling. A number of these trainees had previously been running stress management workshops or counselling stressed individuals with little prior training or in-depth knowledge of the subject. In addition, few of them were receiving regular supervision of their stress-related work. This raises an issue over the quality of service being offered to their clients. Employers may also be unaware that they could be held responsible in law for contracting inexperienced and incompetent practitioners.

Reynolds and Briner (Chapter 11) suggest that most stress management training courses are based on multimodal, cognitive behaviour therapy. They reach this conclusion by studying the published research. However, this probably does not reflect what is actually undertaken in Britain (and perhaps elsewhere) as most trainers, in our experience, have limited competence in this area. In addition most training manuals that are available on the market for the trainer to use (e.g. Cabinet Office, 1987; Clarke, 1989, etc.) do not include cognitive-behavioural interventions apart from standard relaxation exercises. Fortunately this situation has started to change (e.g. Clarke and Palmer, 1994).

Different approaches and the related issues raised in this book will now be discussed.

THE BIOLOGICAL APPROACH TO STRESS MANAGEMENT

In Chapter 2, Gregson and Looker believe that an understanding of the biological basis of stress management may assist counsellors and facilitators in running stress management interventions. From their own experience, they have found that clients wish to learn about the physiological aspects of stress. If the stress management programme includes a physiological rationale then clients are 'more likely to adopt and adhere to a stress management strategy' (p. 19). However, this may be just anecdotal, and formal research to test this hypothesis is needed. In a similar area of work, we have also noted that if stress health education lectures do not include the biological aspects of stress, at question time members of the audience usually raise the topic for discussion. Although this is again anecdotal, as are the views of Gregson and Looker, it has a common sense validity.

Often interventions are consumer led and clients ask for a number of topics to be covered. We find that the most commonly requested subjects chosen by participants attending a series of industrial stress management workshops are: what is stress?; how to recognize stress in self and others; how to deal with stress in self and others; coping strategies; and relaxation techniques. Groups of participants who do not work in a health-related field tend not to ask for a large range of topics but include headings such as coping strategies that may include many specific techniques. If the participants are given a large choice of options beforehand then the requests are more varied and may include whatever is indicated on the possible programme such as assertion training, time management, etc. On most occasions, however, the participants want an explanation of the physiology and causes of stress. Therefore its inclusion within a stress management workshop, lecture, seminar or counselling session would seem necessary if the desires of the typical client group are to be met.

Gregson and Looker believe that an explanation of the biology of stress helps to explain to individuals the relevance of different coping strategies such as the relaxation response, biofeedback, correct breathing and lifestyle changes. Subsequently, they suggest that the 'stress response can be managed more effectively when physiologically based strategies are included as part of the programme' (p. 29).

THE PERSON-CENTRED APPROACH TO STRESS MANAGEMENT

In Chapter 3, Clarke suggests that the 'difference between the person-centred approach and other forms of therapeutic intervention lies in the way the therapist works within the therapeutic encounter, particularly in terms of her or his rejection of an expert position and positive view of acceptance of the client's subjective view of reality' (p. 37). In addition, 'the therapist must have trust in the belief that the client is fundamentally capable of determining his or her own constructive growth' (p. 34). In essence, the person-centred counsellor is less interested in the educational-biological model of Gregson and Looker or the model of Abrams and Ellis (see Chapter 5), but is far more interested in the 'client's personal and subjective attributions of any perceived "problem" ' (p. 37). If necessary, the decision to use a specific stress management technique would be left to the client. This would avoid the counsellor taking the role of the expert.

This raises a number of issues. Unless the layperson client is made aware of the possible interventions or techniques that may be available to manage stress then certain complaints such as phobias, hypertension and compulsive behaviours may not improve. (This assumes that if the client is made aware of the methods the client would then apply them in the desired manner.) If the counsellor does inform the client about exposure programmes and relaxation techniques then the counsellor could be mistaken as an 'expert'. Pharmacotherapy may also be necessary, especially with potentially life-threatening conditions, e.g. essential hypertension. If the counsellor does not have knowledge of these techniques or does not mention them to the client, this could raise ethical issues. Therefore to remain true to a person-centred philosophy a counsellor would need to avoid the 'expert' role and yet be able to help the client explore any issue of their choice, which may include stress management techniques. In practice, this could be difficult unless the counsellor refers the client elsewhere to learn specific skills or techniques and suggests suitable bibliotherapy. But even this from the client's frame of reference could appear as the counsellor taking the role of an expert. Perhaps what cannot be avoided is that clients may perceive all counsellors using any approach as being 'experts' in at least one field, i.e. 'counselling'.

Clarke does not cover person-centred organizational interventions although others have taken the client-centred approach into industry (e.g. Evans and Reynolds, 1993; Palmer, 1993a). Both Evans and Reynolds and Palmer tend to use similar models to engage and work within organizations (see Figure 1.1) but leave the final choice and responsibility to the client for the stress management intervention.

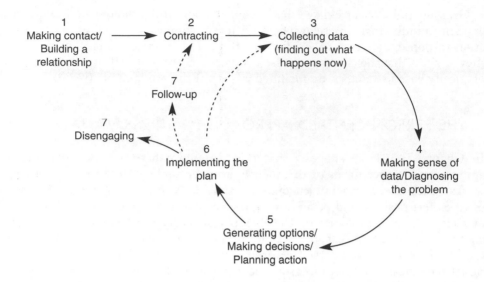

Figure 1.1 *The consulting cycle (from Evans and Reynolds, 1993)*

THE MULTIMODAL APPROACH: THEORY, ASSESSMENT, TECHNIQUES AND INTERVENTIONS

In Chapter 4, Palmer shows how he has adapted the multimodal therapy approach of Lazarus (1981; 1989) to the area of stress counselling and stress management. The approach is underpinned by social learning theory (Bandura, 1977) and mainly uses a wide range of cognitive-behavioural techniques and interventions to help individuals suffering from stress and stress-related symptoms. Palmer and Dryden (1995) adapted the five-stage transactional model of stress developed by Cox (1978) and Cox and Mackay (1981) to incorporate the seven modalities which are used in multimodal therapy to aid assessment of clients: Behaviour, Affect, Sensation, Imagery, Cognition, Interpersonal, and Drugs/Biology. This modality assessment is usually known by the acronym BASIC I.D. If and when necessary, the treatment, counselling or training programme focuses on problems arising in each modality. One of the issues this chapter raises for stress counsellors and practitioners is that to be truly effective, a practitioner would need to be trained in a wide range of techniques and have sufficient knowledge to know when and when not to use these techniques (i.e. the indications and contra-indications) for a given problem and a particular client. This could take extensive training and ongoing supervision which may deter many stress management practitioners who may prefer only to focus on one modality and only teach clients or trainees a few techniques such as relaxation or meditation.

RATIONAL EMOTIVE BEHAVIOUR THERAPY IN THE TREATMENT OF STRESS

The rational emotive behaviour therapy (REBT) approach to the treatment of stress focuses on changing the 'client's philosophies, attitudes and beliefs which lead to disturbance' (see Chapter 5, p. 62). Abrams and Ellis claim that 'stress does not exist *define* in itself' (p. 62). It only exists due to the perceptions and reactions of the individual. However, they do accept that some activating events are so traumatic, e.g. rape, that a large percentage of individuals will upset themselves about the event. *Quote.*

They believe that the prime determinant of stress is the individual's irrational beliefs and self-defeating styles. Irrational beliefs consist of absolutistic, inflexible and dogmatic beliefs and generally come in the form of musts, shoulds, oughts, have tos and got tos. They often have subsequent evaluative conclusions such as 'it is terrible/awful that …' and 'I can't stand it' derivatives. The REBT counsellor or trainer targets these beliefs for disputation and subsequent change. The common disputes used by the counsellor to challenge the client's irrational beliefs are:

1. Logical (e.g. Is this belief logical?)
2. Empirical (e.g. Where is the evidence for the belief?)
3. Pragmatic (e.g. Where is it going to get the person holding on to this belief?)

REBT is multimodal as it may use other techniques such as assertion, reframing, relaxation, biofeedback, social skills training, etc. However, these are still used within the philosophical framework of REBT.

The approach has also been used in organizational settings (e.g. DiMattia, 1991; Miller and Yeager, 1993; Neenan, 1993; Palmer, 1993b; Richman, 1993). The workshop or seminar titles include 'managing pressure to increase performance' and 'rational effectiveness training'.

Whether the approach is used in industry or in counselling, the participant or client soon realizes that they are seen as responsible for their own levels of distress. A typical example that a trainer or counsellor could encounter is an individual who states 'my boss makes me angry'. In this example, the trainer or counsellor would help the individual to see that it was not her boss that made her angry but instead the individual made herself angry about what her boss had done. This subtle difference shifts the responsibility to the client for her anger. Then the individual is shown how her beliefs largely contribute to the emotion of anger. Although this approach may appeal to many individuals, many others refuse to accept that the stressor is not largely responsible for their distress. However, they may still find the other techniques an REBT practitioner uses helpful.

TRAUMATIC STRESS AT WORK: A PUBLIC HEALTH MODEL

In Chapter 6, Richards describes an organizational response to reduce the impact of armed robberies on staff of a national building society. Although traumatic incidents may be an example of extreme stressors, Richards demonstrates how a public health model is applied at primary, secondary and tertiary levels. The organization in question instigated a comprehensive programme which includes pre-raid training right through to cognitive-behavioural counselling if necessary. The programme appears to successfully integrate a health education and a psychotherapeutic approach. In addition, by running a health-monitoring system, more information will become available on the effectiveness of the approach to reduce post-traumatic stress in this at-risk group. At present this is necessary as there is a lack of published research in this field of work that evaluates the commonly used techniques such as debriefing (see Parkinson, 1995). Yet these techniques and methods are being sold by consultants to industry as the panacea.

An outcome study may produce useful information. However, in order to conduct a controlled study, it is necessary that one staff group does *not* receive specific pre- or post-raid intervention(s). This may not be ethical. Another option may be to carry out a study with a similar organization, e.g. another large building society, that does not offer its staff any help, pre- or post-raid. If all similar organizations now offer their staff assistance then the private security industry could possibly be used instead, as the majority of security companies do not offer any support to their staff whatsoever (see Palmer, 1991).

STRESS MANAGEMENT INTERVENTIONS IN THE WORKPLACE: STRESS COUNSELLING AND STRESS AUDITS

In Chapter 7, Cooper and Cartwright state that they believe organizational interventions need to be made at three levels:

- the individual
- the individual/organizational interface
- the organization

However, according to Cooper and Cartwright most interventions are targeted at the individual level and neglect the reduction of organizational stressors or do not provide in-depth stress counselling. A multilevelled assessment and intervention may be necessary. They advocate the use of organizational 'stress audits' which assess the levels of stress in different areas of an organization such as specific jobs and departments. They argue that regular organizational 'stress audits' can provide the information required and a baseline measure for evaluation purposes.

The main problem with stress audits is selling the idea to management. More often than not, in our experience the purchaser(s) of services in an organization prefers to buy a series of stress management workshops or seminars. Unfortunately, the possibly more useful options such as stress audits, stress counselling and Employee Assistance Programmes are considered expensive. Unlike stress audits, training workshops are a relatively cheap option that may not necessarily prevent or reduce stress in a non-clinical group of individuals. Yet these workshops may initially give the appearance of a caring organization whereas in reality it is only going through the motions. The major question is how do you educate purchasers that a stress audit would be a sensible place to start the stress management programme? Perhaps conclusive evidence that stress management interventions can

good

reduce sickness absence (e.g. Allison *et al.*, 1989) would act as an incentive. However, during the recession, for many organizations the financial constraints will restrict their choice of intervention(s). Fortunately, in some organizations where Total Quality Management circles are being established, the issue of stress can be raised by the staff and an in-house stress audit may become practicable.

positive organisation for employee

More recently, the court verdict in favour of the plaintiff, *John Walker v. Northumberland Council*, in which Walker was awarded damages for occupational stress, has increased the level of interest employers are giving to stress (see Palmer, 1995). In addition, a government body, the Health and Safety Executive, has now developed guidelines for employers on dealing with stress at work (Health and Safety Executive, 1995). The court verdict and the guidelines may encourage employers to adopt a more thorough approach to stress management and subsequently turn their attention to organizationally-focused interventions and not just symptom management.

It is a must now due to the new law on Health & Safety.

STRESS MANAGEMENT APPROACHES TO THE PREVENTION OF CORONARY HEART DISEASE

In Chapter 8, Bennett and Carroll review the effectiveness of stress management techniques in reducing three known risk factors for coronary heart disease (CHD): Type A behaviour (TAB), raised serum cholesterol and hypertension. This chapter provides a key review of the many research papers which clearly indicate that stress management techniques can reduce the risk associated with the three risk factors. An important observation is that just one type of intervention may effectively lower three independent risk factors for CHD. However, the authors do point out that in some cases self-management methods may be more suitable for interventions related to weight loss and smoking.

Probably one of the most interesting propositions put forward by Bennett and Carroll is the development of community-wide interventions targeted at stress reduction. They also suggest that the teaching of stress management techniques via the mass media could be a useful preventive strategy. This could include televised stress management courses, community education courses and bibliotherapy.

INDIVIDUAL STRATEGIES FOR COPING WITH STRESS AT WORK: A REVIEW

In Chapter 9, Dewe, Cox and Ferguson raise a number of methodological and conceptual issues involved in research on coping. By examining 17 recent papers, they identify four issues which should be considered in future research: the need to distinguish between coping style and coping behaviour in relation to the instructions used in measurement scales; the use of composite multi-item scales to note a particular type of coping; having to decide between occupationally specific or more general coping measures in connection with the focus of the scale or instrument; and the meaning individuals give to events and to the measurement of that meaning. With particular reference to the last point, Dewe *et al.* conclude that stress and coping should be defined and measured within the framework of a transactional approach.

In Chapter 4, Palmer demonstrated how the transactional approach can be adapted to a multimodal framework for preventive stress management or stress counselling (see multimodal-transactional model of stress, pp. 47–9). However, O'Driscoll and Cooper in Chapter 10 suggest an alternative methodology that can be used with some of the problems raised in Chapter 9.

COPING WITH WORK-RELATED STRESS: A CRITIQUE OF EXISTING MEASURES AND A PROPOSAL FOR AN ALTERNATIVE METHODOLOGY

In Chapter 10, O'Driscoll and Cooper have focused on some of the methodological difficulties encountered in research on coping with stress, such as the limitations inherent in the existing coping measures. They concur with Edwards (1988) that our understanding of the stress-coping process remains incomplete. Perhaps two of the key questions are: 'How do individuals deal with or manage the stress they experience?' and 'What are effective methods of coping with work-related stress?'

O'Driscoll and Cooper have proposed a framework known as critical incident analysis (CIA) for the assessment of coping with work-related stressors. CIA was first described by Flanagan (1954) and has a number of advantages in the investigation of stress-coping strategies: it has an ecological validity of information about individuals' responses in specific situations; it should ensure a more accurate account of the specific behaviours which individuals exhibit in response to stressful events; and it should provide a closer examination of the outcomes of situationally-specific coping behaviours. Although CIA has a number of potential difficulties, it does offer a methodology for linking coping behaviours to sources of stress in work settings which may eventually lead to a greater understanding about the stress-coping process. This may deal with some of the problems raised in Chapter 9.

STRESS MANAGEMENT AT WORK: WITH WHOM, FOR WHOM AND TO WHAT ENDS?

Reynolds and Briner (Chapter 11) have raised many important issues regarding the entire field of stress management interventions. They are concerned that a stress management industry has developed that 'attempts to alleviate the supposed effects of occupational stress' (p. 144). They argue that group stress management training and individual counselling services should be seen as two distinctive interventions with 'different aims, different participants, and different possible outcomes, each of which should influence the design of evaluation research'. In addition, their analysis of the research suggests that there is a lack of evidence to support the link between individual well-being and organizational outcomes. They also suggest that the existing research does not indicate that stress management training inoculates the individual from physical and chronic mental disorder.

To complicate the issue further, even if an assessment or stress audit recommends that the preferred intervention would be a multimodal, cognitive-behavioural stress management workshop, will the organization employ a competent cognitive-behavioural practitioner? Unfortunately, in our experience 'positive thinking' is often incorrectly mistaken for cognitive disputation and reappraisal. We suggest that organizations should employ stress management practitioners who have adequate knowledge and competency in the following areas:

- adequate competency in cognitive-behavioural techniques
- adequate competency in rational emotive behavioural techniques
- adequate competency in counselling and listening skills
- adequate competency in group facilitation skills
- adequate competency in teaching related key topics
- adequate competency in problem-solving skills/training
- adequate competency in the use of psychometric tests
- knowledge of relevant research
- knowledge of lifestyle options, e.g. diet, exercise, etc.
- understanding of occupational, organizational, change, management, family, social and cultural issues

The existing research literature seldom includes information on the assessed competencies of the stress management facilitator or counsellor. Also the competencies of the assessors would need to be published. Even if the facilitator or counsellor is a qualified psychologist, how many occupational psychologists also have adequate clinical skills and vice versa? Interestingly, the existing research literature that looks at different cognitive-behavioural techniques used in clinical settings also tends to neglect the therapeutic skills and experience of the therapist.

CONCLUSION

The papers for this book were chosen to illustrate the practice of stress management, without neglecting the theory, research and methodological issues involved. The emphasis on coping research was not coincidental as we believe that many stress management practitioners do not understand the problems surrounding coping research even though they may teach their clients so-called 'effective' coping strategies.

Unfortunately, in the past decade, the methodological problems and the lack of systematic evaluation of organizational stress management interventions have been largely ignored. However, there have been fewer methodological problems in connection with the research focusing on individuals with stress-related symptoms such as CHD.

The well-known Life Events Rating Scale developed by Holmes and Rahe (1967) did not take into account an individual's perception of events and was later challenged (see Cooper et al., 1988) as it led to inconsistent results. For the very same reason, if the internal demands of an individual, e.g. 'I must perform well at all times' (see Abrams and Ellis, Chapter 5), are not brought into the complex equation then organizational stress management assessments and interventions will not necessarily target one of the crucial sources of stress. As long as one person's stressor is another person's challenge, interventions in this field of work will probably continue to be difficult to evaluate, especially within an organizational setting. The transactional model of stress focuses on this person–environment fit, yet this perspective has not been integrated into current measurement practice, even less into the applied practice of stress management. Still the most usual approach to stress management or stress counselling is reactive symptom management, e.g. relaxation training, and not the more proactive appraisal training (see cognitive techniques in Chapters 4 and 5) or organizational change interventions.

The papers chosen have highlighted a number of key issues that both researchers and practitioners need to consider when undertaking research or interventions in the field of stress management.

REFERENCES

Allison, T., Cooper, C.L. and Reynolds, P. (1989) Stress counselling in the workplace. *The Psychologist*, 384–88.

Bandura, A. (1977) *Social Learning Theory*. Englewood Cliffs, NJ: Prentice-Hall.

Cabinet Office (1987) *Understanding Stress, Part 3, Trainer Guide*. London: HMSO.

Clarke, D. (1989) *The Effective Trainer Series. Stress Management*. Cambridge: National Extension College.

Clarke, D. and Palmer, S. (1994) *Stress Management*. Cambridge: National Extension College.

Cooper, C., Cooper, R. and Eaker, L. (1988) *Living with Stress*. Harmondsworth: Penguin.

Cox, T. (1978) *Stress*. London: Macmillan.

Cox, T. and Mackay, C.J. (1981) A transactional approach to occupational stress. In E.N. Corlett and J. Richardson (eds), *Stress, Work Design and Productivity*. Chichester: Wiley.

DiMattia, D.D. (1991) Using RET effectively in the workplace. In M.E. Bernard (ed.), *Using Rational-Emotive Therapy Effectively: A Practitioner's Guide*. London: Plenum Press.

Edwards, J. (1988) The determinants and consequences of coping with stress. In C. Cooper and R. Payne (eds), *Causes, Coping and Consequences of Stress at Work*, pp. 233–63. Chichester: Wiley.

Evans, B. and Reynolds, P. (1993) Stress consulting: A client centred approach. *Stress News* 5:1, 2–6.

Flanagan, J. (1954) The criticial incident technique. *Psychological Bulletin*, **51**, 327–58.

Health and Safety Executive (1995) *Stress at Work: A Guide for Employers*. Sudbury: HSE.

Holmes, T.H. and Rahe, R.H. (1967) The social readjustment rating scale. *Journal of Psychomatic Research*, **11**, 213–18.

Lazarus, A.A. (1981) *The Practice of Multimodal Therapy*. New York: McGraw-Hill.

Lazarus, A.A. (1989) *The Practice of Multimodal Therapy*. Baltimore, MD: The Johns Hopkins University Press.

Miller, A.R. and Yeager, R.J. (1993) Managing change: A corporate application of Rational-Emotive Therapy. *Journal of Rational-Emotive & Cognitive Behavior Therapy*, **11**:2, 65–76.

Neenan, M. (1993) Rational-Emotive Therapy at work. *Stress News*, **5**:1, 7–10.

Palmer, S. (1991) Stress, health, safety and welfare in the security industry. *The Safety and Health Practitioner*, October, 14–17.

Palmer, S. (1993a) Stress management interventions. *The Specialist (International)*, **4**:6, 35–9.

Palmer, S. (1993b) The 'Deserted Island Technique': A method of demonstrating how preferential and musturbatory beliefs can lead to different emotions. *The Rational-Emotive Therapist*, **1**:1, 12–14.

Palmer, S. (1995) Legal aspects of occupational stress. *Counselling Psychology Review*, **10**:4, 18–21.

Palmer, S. and Dryden, W. (1995) *Counselling for Stress Problems*. London: Sage.

Parkinson, F. (1995) Critical incident debriefing. *Counselling, Journal of the British Association for Counselling*, **6**:3, 186–7.

Richman, D.R. (1993) Cognitive career counselling: A rational-emotive approach to career development. *Journal of Rational-Emotive & Cognitive-Behavior Therapy*, **11**:2, 91–108.

PART TWO
Biological Basis of Stress Management

CHAPTER 2

The Biological Basis of Stress Management

Olga Gregson and Terry Looker

A rationale is outlined for the inclusion of a biological approach in stress management programmes. The biology of the stress response is described in sufficient detail to show the layperson what happens in the body when stress is experienced. An explanation of the biological basis of commonly used coping strategies is given.

INTRODUCTION

It is the purpose of this chapter to outline how we believe counsellors and facilitators may benefit from knowledge about the biology of stress to assist their stress management programmes. Understanding the biology of stress can help in the following ways:

1. The subject is of intrinsic interest. Most individuals are curious about how their body works and what can happen as a result of distress.
2. Such knowledge raises awareness, allowing the individual to rationalize a particular therapy, thereby promoting its effectiveness.
3. Such knowledge can be used as a form of therapy in its own right, empowering the individual to deal with stress by helping to describe and explain:

   - The signs and symptoms of stress.
   - How distress can lead to ill-health.
   - The physiological changes that accompany emotions and behaviour.
   - The pharmacological basis of treatment for stress-related disorders.
   - The rationale of coping strategies such as relaxation training; the need to encourage social support; the need for lifestyle changes and anger control.

RATIONALE

There is a growing realization that the subject of stress is best approached as a 'construct': that stress can be regarded as a synthesis of several interacting approaches. An analogy may be made here with the story of the three blind men describing an elephant. The blind man who touched the elephant's ear said it was like a fan. Another who touched its trunk said it was obvious that it was like a thick rope. And so on. Each blind man was convinced that his description was the right one. What was needed was for them to put their descriptions together and co-operate in providing a much broader view of the subject as a whole.

This chapter is an attempt to show how such an outcome can be achieved. As physiologists, we can compare ourselves with one of the 'blind men', offering a particular approach to the study of stress. By illustrating the biology of the stress response, we can suggest ways in which our knowledge can be linked with other approaches to address the subject of stress and its management from a much broader perspective and from an eclectic point of view.

A framework in which to explain a physiological approach is based on the model of stress proposed by Kagan and Levi (1974). Our simplified model shown in Figure 2.1 describes stress as a whole-body-and-mind interactive response to a demand or pressure (stressor). Viewed in this way, stress is experienced as a state in which the body, the mind and their interaction with the environment can all be targeted for modification within a stress management programme as outlined in Figure 2.2.

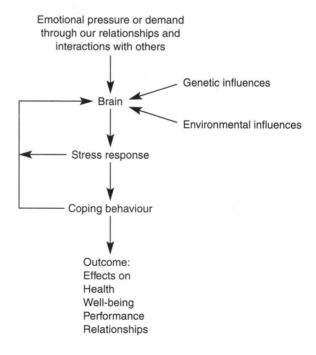

Figure 2.1 *A model of the stress response*

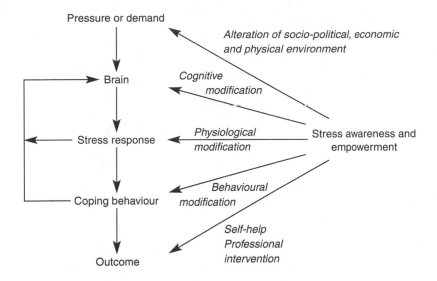

Figure 2.2 *A model of stress management*

Understanding the biology of stress can significantly enhance the effectiveness of therapy. From our own stress management programmes we have found that individuals are very interested to know what is actually happening physiologically. They are more likely to adopt and adhere to a stress management strategy if the reasons for the proposed strategy are explained in a way that includes a physiological rationale.

Focus on the stress response tends to be the predominant approach to the study of stress by physiologists, based on the views of Selye (1956). Although Selye's work is still influential, it is now recognized that his views are too narrow and inaccurate in the light of more recent research (Henry, 1986). Nevertheless, a physiological viewpoint, in which stress is regarded as a whole-body-mind response, may be one which counsellors and stress management practitioners have considered least. What follows is very much an oversimplification of actual events during the stress response; from our experience, however, this is sufficient to enable the layperson to understand the biological basis of this response, together with the implications for stress management (Looker and Gregson, 1989).

BIOLOGY OF THE STRESS RESPONSE

To understand the stress response we need to focus on the main 'stress chemicals': adrenaline, noradrenaline and cortisol. The response to a stressor is determined by the brain, resulting in the release of a specific 'cocktail' of these 'stress chemicals' (Figure 2.3) to bring about the appropriate bodily responses. This leads to some form of behaviour or psychophysiological response, for dealing with the stressor. Actually, the interpretive processes in the brain rely entirely on biochemical reactions between the nerve cells, so the stress response is initiated the instant the stressor is detected by our senses.

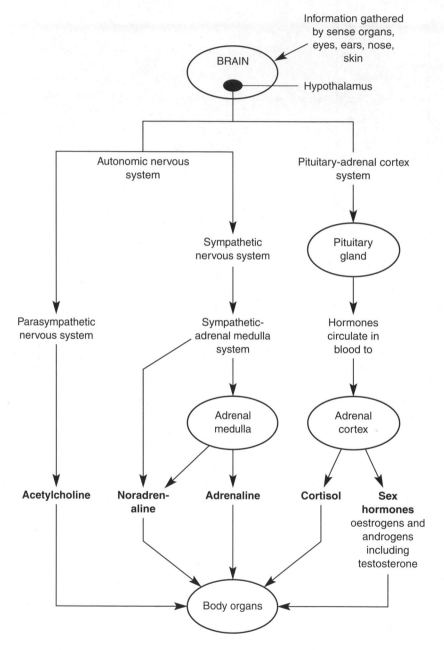

Figure 2.3 *Biological mechanism of the stress response*

Once sensory receptors have relayed information about the stressor to the brain, the signals are processed to give meaning and awareness of the stressor. Past experience or memory influence the perceptual processes. The cortex, the part of the brain where the 'highest' level of processing occurs, generates further signals to various parts of the body. The stress response is 'geared' emotionally, provided by another part of the brain (the limbic system), and has a drive strength (motivation). Structures in the limbic system, especially the part called the amygdala, are associated with the emotions of fear, anxiety and anger. Emotions organize or 'colour' the response decided in the cortex.

Whatever action the brain decides should be taken, the body must be prepared for the corresponding type and level of physical activity. This process of preparation is mainly the role of another structure in the brain – the hypothalamus. This acts through the autonomic nervous system (ANS) and the endocrine system, to organize the body's physiological responses.

The response to the stressor by the body is ultimately achieved by altering the activity of the body organs, thus enabling the body to deal with the situation through some form of action or behaviour. It is the job of the 'stress chemicals' to alter body-organ activity. Different chemicals and various patterns of activation produce different effects: for instance, one chemical speeds the heart beat, while another decreases the heart rate. The interpretive processes in the brain determine the type of chemical messengers and 'mixture' to be released on to the body organs to produce the end response.

Instructions, in the form of electrical signals from the hypothalamus to the body, are carried along nerves. Especially important in the stress response are the nerves that form the ANS. This part of the nervous system, as the name implies, works to ensure that vital body processes – such as heart beating, breathing and digestion – work automatically, do not stop, and are adjusted accordingly with changing conditions imposed by the stressor. The ANS is in fact two systems: the sympathetic (SNS) and the parasympathetic (PNS) nervous systems. There are those who believe that the three main 'stress chemicals' activate the body responses through increased activity in the SNS with a corresponding decrease in PNS activity. Cannon (1927) describes this pattern in detail. The manifestations of this response, preparing the body for action through either 'fight' or 'flight', are well known. Others, since James (1884), believe that the pattern of response by the ANS corresponds specifically to the nature of the interpretive processes made by the cortex and intensified by the limbic system. There is no question that Cannon's 'emergency response' is one pattern that the ANS can produce. There is much evidence, however, that the ANS is capable of a number of different patterns of activation (Sokolov, 1963). Knowing about ANS specificity is important in helping to understand the links between specific emotions and stress management. For example, there is now evidence which suggests that individuals prone to distress may have an ANS in which the PNS activity appears to be reduced below normal, resulting in exaggerated SNS activity (Hausken et al., 1993).

Recognizing, and being able to manage the expression of stress response activity, is in itself a coping strategy if the emotional and behavioural signs are heeded. Most body organs receive messages from both divisions of the ANS. Table 2.1 shows some of the body actions brought about by SNS and PNS activity.

Actions of the nervous system are largely brought about by chemicals, known as neurotransmitters because they transmit messages from the nerve ending to an organ.

ORGAN/TISSUE	Parasympathetic effect	Sympathetic effect
Heart	Decreased rate	Increased rate and force of beat
Blood vessels	Generally little or no effect but can cause dilation (widening) of blood vessels to heart muscle, lungs, brain and sex organs	Constrict except those supplying heart, leg and arm muscles, which dilate
Spleen	–	Contracts and empties stored red blood cells into the circulation
Salivary glands	Increased flow of saliva	Decreased flow of saliva
Gut muscles	Increased movement	Decreased movement
Lung airways	Constrict, decreasing air flow	Dilate, increasing air flow
Sweat glands	–	Increased sweating
Pupils of eye	Contraction of sphincter muscle of iris; pupil becomes smaller – constricts	Contraction of radial muscle of iris; pupil becomes wider – dilates
Liver and fat tissue	–	Mobilization of sugar and fat
Brain, mental activity	–	Mental activity increased
Blood	–	Increased ability to clot

(–) = little or no effect

TABLE 2.1 *Actions of the autonomic nervous system*

Actions of the SNS are as a result of the release of a neurotransmitter called noradrenaline, whereas PNS action is mainly brought about by the neurotransmitter acetylcholine. When electrical signals arrive at the end of a nerve from the brain, small amounts of neurotransmitter are released from the ends of the nerve on to receptor sites in the membranes of the cells which form the body organs. Neurotransmitters alter the activity of the organ by switching chemical reactions 'on' or 'off' in the organ.

Another way in which chemical messages reach the organs is via the blood stream, in the form of hormones released from endocrine glands. Endocrine glands are specialized organs that manufacture and release hormones in response to signals from the nervous system.

Of special importance in the stress response are the adrenal glands. There are two adrenal glands, one on top of each kidney, which are the source of several hormones released during the stress response. Each adrenal gland consists of two parts, each a distinct gland in its own right. The central part of the gland, the medulla, produces two hormones, adrenaline and noradrenaline. The hormone noradrenaline is the same chemical as the neurotransmitter noradrenaline released at the SNS nerve endings. The significance of this is described below. The SNS supplies nerves to the adrenal medulla and controls the release of both adrenaline and noradrenaline. Although the names adrenaline and noradrenaline sound as though the chemicals are similar (both belong to a group of chemicals known as catecholamines), they are quite distinct in their chemical structure and each affects the body organs differently. This distinction is important since the body is prepared for either fighting or fleeing through the release of different cocktails of these two chemicals (see Table 2.2).

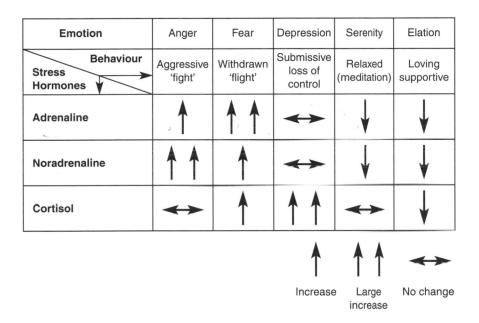

Table 2.2 *Changes in stress hormones related to emotions and behaviours*

The adrenal cortex, the outer part of the adrenal gland, produces several hormones to prepare the body to deal more with long-term demands. One of these hormones is cortisol. The actions of the stress hormones are summarized in Table 2.3.

The stress response involves the release of many neurotransmitters and hormones to initiate and maintain the body's response for as long as the stressor persists. Each chemical triggers a different set of actions in the body's organs involving most if not all of the body systems. Noradrenaline, for example, is released as a neurotransmitter, to

Table 2.3 Effects of adrenaline/noradrenaline and cortisol

Adrenaline and noradrenaline	
Heart:	increased rate and force of beat
Blood vessels:	constrict in skin and internal organs; dilate in body muscle, lungs, brain
Blood:	clots more easily and more quickly
Spleen:	discharges more oxygen carrying red blood cells into circulation
Lungs:	air passages dilate; breathing becomes deeper and more rapid
Glucose and fat stores:	mobilized for source of energy
Skin:	sweating occurs; tactile sensitivity increased; 'goose pimples' appear
Digestive system:	activity reduced
Senses:	sensitivity increases; pupils dilate; vision, smell and hearing become more acute
Cortisol	
Glucose and fat mobilization	
Sensitizes the immune system	
Reduces inflammatory response	
Reduces allergic reaction	

initiate organ action, and as a hormone to prolong and maintain the same organ action. This course of activity is necessary because of the way in which the nervous system and endocrine system operate. The nervous system produces signals that are rapidly transmitted to initiate a body response, but these nerve impulses are short-lived. The endocrine system can be viewed as an extension of the nervous system. Signals from the nervous system to the endocrine glands result in the release of hormones which pass on the message from the nervous system by circulating in the blood to their target organs. It clearly takes a little while for hormones to reach their target organ so, in this way, hormones effectively prolong and maintain organ response which the neurotransmitter has initiated.

The stress response is a necessary and normal response to change, or even lack of change. However, some changes signal danger (we may experience distress) whilst others are enjoyable (we experience eustress). It is not yet clear which pattern of stress response activation occurs during the various experiences or states of distress or eustress. Most of what is known deals with the experience of distress. More research is needed into the physiology of eustress.

TYPE A BEHAVIOUR

One of the most significant manifestations of the stress response is seen in the individual's relationship with the outside world through their behaviour. Understanding the links between ANS activity and behaviour can assist in stress management, since behaviour reflects what is happening in the mind and body. A specific pattern of behaviour, known as Type A behaviour (TAB) (Friedman and Rosenman, 1974), is regarded as a maladaptive coping behaviour which appears to be highly relevant to the development of coronary heart disease. Individuals who display extreme Type A behaviour hold beliefs by which they strive to stay in control of everything, all of the time. They engage in a continuous struggle to achieve more and more in less and less time, frequently in the face of opposition, real or imagined, from other persons. This often results in irritability, impatience and aggressiveness, frequently over apparently trivial events.

Research has shown that those who display Type A behaviour have enhanced noradrenaline and adrenaline secretion, with excessive noradrenaline release during bouts of anger (Chesney and Rosenman, 1985). The pattern of noradrenaline release appears to result from enhanced SNS stress response activation compared with those who manifest Type B behaviour: the 'opposite' of Type A behaviour. The characteristics of Type B behaviour include being patient, not rushed and not getting irritated over trivial situations and events. Fuming in a traffic jam releases too much noradrenaline. Without the ability to express the natural accompanying behaviour, accidents are more likely to occur as tempers become frayed. For those living in the Type A inducing mode, it is not surprising to see many of the signs and symptoms of distress.

Understanding the biology of the stress response can assist Type A behaviour modification in stress management by looking at *how not to* activate the SNS stress response. For example, anger control and moderating the intake of SNS activity enhancers, such as caffeine, will result in less SNS arousal, and therefore in less noradrenaline being released.

THE STRESS RESPONSE, HEALTH AND WELL-BEING

The ultimate outcome of stress response reactivity is the effect on health and well-being. For example, overactivation of the stress response for prolonged periods, and/or frequent and/or intense activation of the stress response, will clearly lead to over-stimulation, in some way, of the body organs and systems. As a result, minor disorders and diseases may arise: physical, mental and behavioural. Because the response involves the whole body, there are many signs of distress, and related disorders and diseases (Tables 2.4 and 2.5).

Care must be taken in interpreting the signs of stress since many can be due to other factors, such as cold weather giving rise to constriction of the skin blood vessels resulting in cool skin. Redistribution of blood flow here is due to temperature effects and not the stress response. Signs such as back and neck pain, headaches, muscular aches and pains, spasms and cramps, constipation, diarrhoea, indigestion and nausea can all arise for reasons other than stress response overactivation. It is when a number of signs and symptoms occur together and/or more frequently, that they may be attributed to stress response effects.

A further point to emphasize is that not all of the actions of the stress response can be seen outwardly. These 'hidden' signs, such as changes in blood fat and

Table 2.4 *Signs of distress*

Awareness of heart beating, palpitations
Breathlessness, lump in the throat, rapid shallow breathing
Dry mouth, 'butterflies' in stomach, indigestion, nausea
Diarrhoea, constipation, flatulence
General muscle tenseness particularly of the jaws, grinding of teeth
Clenched fists, hunched shoulders, general muscle aches and pains, cramps
Restless, hyperactive, nail biting, finger drumming, foot tapping, hands shaking
Tired, fatigued, lethargic, exhausted, sleep difficulties, feeling faint, headaches
Frequent illnesses such as colds
Sweaty especially palms and upper lip, hot flushed feeling
Cold hands and feet
Frequent desire to urinate
Overeating, loss of appetite, increased cigarette smoking
Increased alcohol consumption, loss of interest in sex

Table 2.5 *Some distress-related diseases*

Coronary heart disease (angina and heart attacks)
Hypertension (high blood pressure)
Strokes
Migraine
Indigestion
Heartburn
Stomach and duodenal ulcers
Ulcerative colitis
Irritable bowel syndrome
Headaches
Diabetes
Cancers
Rheumatoid arthritis
Allergies
Asthma
Common cold and flu

glucose levels and increased ability of the blood to clot, are also present. Since stress is a whole-body response, the 'stress chemicals' can be used as a reliable marker of stress. Taking measurements from the blood can provide an index of 'unseen' physiological responses as well as an index of psychological and emotional states associated with stress (Table 2.2).

Understanding the biology of the stress response explains how ill-health arises through its excessive and/or frequent activation. For example, it is claimed that the high levels of noradrenaline produced during aggressive behaviour can lead to a heart attack through a number of mechanisms, involving plaque rupture, coronary thrombosis, coronary spasm and initiation of fatal arrhythmias. Excessive cate-cholamine production has also been implicated in the development of coronary atherosclerosis (Haft, 1974; Dimsdale and Moss, 1980; Wright, 1988).

Cortisol, too, has been implicated in ill-health. There is now much evidence to show that excessive release of cortisol, over a period of time, can overtax the immune system. The less serious consequence of this is the increased tendency for individuals to suffer from colds and minor infections more frequently. A more serious consequence is the increased susceptibility of individuals to develop cancer and other life-threatening diseases (Society of Behavioural Medicine, 1987).

Why is it that a response that has evolved to save life and improve performance ends up actually making us ill and less efficient, and can become a potential killer? The answer in brief, we believe, is that the stress response has evolved primarily to preserve our lives in the face of life-threatening situations in a different type of envi-ronment. It was ideal for the threats and challenges faced by our ancestors, but today we face different types as well as an increased number of threats and challenges. Dangers such as an attack by a wild animal are rare. Rather, we live in a society where complex social and emotional interactions are now the norm. The threats we perceive are to our self-esteem and to the security of our relationships and jobs. In our daily encounters it is often inappropriate for us to physically 'fight' or 'flee' as the emergency response intended.

Homo sapiens has existed for around 40,000 years in essentially the same biolog-ical form. The urbanized, industrialized high technology era in which we live is a relatively recent event in evolutionary terms. This has presented the greatest variety and amount of change to *Homo sapiens* in a relatively short space of time. We face the consequences of ill-health, poor performance, disrupted relationships and possi-bly death as a result of 'mis-use' of our stress response. Excessive, prolonged and/or frequent activation of the stress response clearly taxes the organ systems as they respond to their chemical instructions. The social rules of our civilized world discourage physical attack or withdrawal. The individual is left in an aroused state with no channel through which to express natural accompanying behavioural responses. This has clear implications for our health, performance and relation-ships.

It would seem that we are at the 'mercy' of our 'stress chemicals': that we have no choice but to react to our environmental demands in a way that imposes physiologi-cal penalties, such as coronary heart disease, on those unfortunate enough to face high demands and pressures. It would seem that the manifestation of Type A behav-iour appears as a consequence of a high-pressured physiological state. Here the physiological evidence may appear to favour such an argument. What we have illus-trated, however, is that the stress response is a mind–body interaction the nature of which is determined by the beliefs we hold about our world. The human animal is capable of rational thought and can make choices. Reasoning results in an appropri-ate 'optimal' stress response. Irrational thought results in the inappropriate use of the stress response. Achieving a rational frame of mind can be enhanced by the inclusion of education about the biology of the stress response in a stress manage-ment programme.

THE BIOLOGICAL BASIS OF COPING STRATEGIES

It is beyond the scope of this chapter to describe the biological basis of stress management in detail. This can be found in Looker and Gregson (1989). A knowledge of the biology of the stress response is, however, extremely relevant for explaining commonly recommended coping strategies – for example:

- the physiology of the relaxation response;
- biofeedback for relaxation training;
- the importance of correct breathing (Fried, 1993);
- the need for certain lifestyle changes.

One of two examples are given here to illustrate this approach.

During relaxation, the activity of the ANS is altered in such a way that the hypothalamus signals a reduction in sympathetic, and an increase in parasympathetic, nervous system activity. In this way the stress response is 'quietened'. Relaxation techniques have been used successfully by clinicians to treat patients with hypertension and high cholesterol levels without the use of medication (e.g. Patel, 1984). Relaxation of the body and of the mind is a powerful stress management strategy which can be explained adequately in terms of its biological basis.

The need for certain lifestyle changes can also be explained within the context of the stress response. The following serve as examples:

- Caffeine stimulates the production of noradrenaline and adrenaline. A person drinking coffee is activating their stress response. Someone who is distressed and drinking coffee is overactivating their stress response.
- A high dietary fat intake, added to the elevated blood fat levels produced during SNS arousal, can lead to excessively high blood fat levels.
- Vitamins and minerals are required for the synthesis of the 'stress chemicals', so during prolonged states of stress these nutrients can become depleted leading to adverse effects on health. Supplements can, therefore, be useful during periods of high demands and pressures.
- Exercise burns up the energy products of the stress response. Regular exercise can beneficially alter the blood fat profiles, resulting in higher amounts of 'good' cholesterol (high-density lipoprotein cholesterol or HDL) and less 'bad' cholesterol (low-density lipoprotein cholesterol or LDL).
- Nicotine stimulates the production of the catecholamines, particularly noradrenaline. The combined effects of smoking and stress lead to significantly higher stress response activation than is achieved through either smoking or stress on their own.

EXPLAINING PHARMACOLOGICAL TREATMENTS

In addition to explaining some of the ways of dealing with stress within a biological framework, common pharmacological treatments for stress can also be explained. For example, the administration of a beta-blocker, such as the drug propranolol, acts to prevent noradrenaline and adrenaline triggering the physiological responses shown in Table 2.1. During administration of the drug, the SNS response occurs as usual and the stress chemicals noradrenaline and adrenaline are released, but their action is prevented by the beta-blocker which occupies the same receptor sites on the body tissues which the catecholamines would occupy. The drug is manufactured in such a way that it is chemically similar enough to be accepted by the receptor site. However, it is chemically different to the catecholamines. As a result, the organs are not activated as much as by the stress chemicals. So in the presence of a beta-blocker, the heart rate does not increase as much (Durel *et al.*, 1985).

The effects of such drugs can be useful to a highly distressed individual, in the short term, in that the pharmacological effect of the beta-blocker (reducing heart rate) can also act as a form of biofeedback. Someone who is anxious will be aware of their 'pounding' heart. The sound and 'feel' of the 'racing' heart can act as a 'distressor', resulting in even more anxiety. This series of events effectively sets up a vicious circle. The beta-blocker can break this self-destructive circle when the heart rate becomes reduced through the drug action. The individual feels less anxious since they can no longer detect an increased and pounding heart-beat. A reduced heart rate signals less arousal. It is also important to know that a less aroused state can be achieved naturally, without the use of drugs, through relaxation therapy.

CONCLUSION

The stress response can be managed more effectively when physiologically based strategies are included as part of the programme. In considering the World Health Organisation (1974) definition of health – 'the mental, physical, social and spiritual well-being of an individual' – stress management strategies ought to be extended to include not only ones based in human biology, but also those which embrace the holistic nature of our well-being.

REFERENCES

Cannon, W.B. (1927) The James-Lange theory of emotions: A critical examination and an alternative theory. *American Journal Psychology*, **39**, 106–24.

Chesney, M.A. and Rosenman, R.H. (1985) *Anger and Hostility in Cardiovascular and Behavioural Disorders.* Washington: Hemisphere.

Dimsdale, J.E. and Moss, J. (1980) Plasma catecholamines in stress and exercise. *Journal of the American Medical Association*, **243**, 340–2.

Durel, L.A., Krantz, D.S., Eisold, J.R. and Lazar, J.D.L. (1985) Behavioural effects of beta blockers: Reduction of anxiety, acute stress and Type A behaviour. *Journal Cardiopulmonary Rehabilitation*, **5**, 267–73.

Fried, R. (1993) *The Psychology and Physiology of Breathing.* New York: Plenum Press.

Friedman, M. and Rosenman, R.H. (1974) *Type A Behaviour and Your Heart*. London: Wildwood House.

Haft, J.I. (1974) Cardiovascular injury induced by sympathetic catecholamines. *Progress in Cardiovascular Diseases*, **17**, 73–86.

Hausken, T., Svebak, S., Wilhelmsen, I., Hang, T.T., Olafsen, K., Petersson, E., Hueem, K. and Berstad, A. (1993) Low vagal tone and antral dysmotility in patients with functional dyspepsia. *Psychosomatic Medicine*, **55**, 12–22.

Henry, J.P. (1986) Neuroendocrine patterns of emotional response. In R. Plutchik and H. Kellerman (eds) *Emotion: Theory and Research, Vol. 3, Biological Foundations of Emotion*. London: Academic Press.

James, W. (1884) What is emotion? *Mind*, **9**, 188–205.

Kagan, A.R. and Levi, L. (1974) Health and environment – psychosocial stimuli: A review. *Society of Science and Medicine*, **8**, 225–41.

Looker, T. and Gregson, O. (1989) *Stresswise: A Practical Guide for Dealing with Stress*. Sevenoaks: Hodder & Stoughton.

Patel, C. (1984) A holistic approach to cardiovascular diseases. *British Journal of Holistic Medicine*, **1**, 30–41.

Selye, H. (1956) *The Stress of Life*. New York: McGraw-Hill.

Society of Behavioural Medicine (1987) Psychoneuroimmunology area review. *Annals of Behavioural Medicine*, **9**, 3–20.

Sokolov, E.N. (1963) Higher nervous functions: The orienting reflex. *Annual Review Physiology*, **25**, 545–80.

World Health Organisation (1974) A/27 Technical discussion.

Wright, L. (1988) The Type A behaviour pattern and coronary artery disease. *American Psychologist*, **43**, 2–14.

PART THREE
Theory and Practice of Stress Management and Counselling

CHAPTER 3

A Person-centred Approach to Stress Management

Peter T. Clarke

Stress is analysed from a phenomenological perspective in terms of how individuals evalute the varying stressors in their lives. The basic philosophical tenets underlying the person-centred approach to therapy are outlined with its emphasis on the ability of the individual human organisms to heal and recover from dysfunction.

INTRODUCTION

The very notion that there might be a person-centred approach to the actual management of stress appears, superficially at least, to be contradictory. How can an approach to therapy, which purports to be non-directive, attempt to 'manage' an individual in his or her attempts to confront such problems as might arise? In effect it is not the person-centred therapist who does the managing, but rather it is the individual client, in an open and accepting relationship with the therapist, who is empowered to take control over his or her own healing. Healing is then seen as an essential personal rather than a technical process (Barnard, 1984) in which the therapist is encountered, not as a diagnostician or technical expert, but rather as a companion to the client in the journey of understanding the subjective reality of the dysfunction.

THE ESSENTIAL NATURE OF THE PERSON-CENTRED APPROACH

Based on the extensive writings of Carl Rogers, the person-(client-)centred approach has become one of the major therapeutic models in use today. At its core is constructive personality change and how the therapist can facilitate this. It is specifically not a directive therapy but it tries to influence the unfolding of the client's experiences in a non-threatening way and without covert or, indeed, overt manipulation. 'The central principle here is that the experiencing of the client has to remain the continuous touchstone for what is introduced by the therapist' (Lietaer, 1990, p. 33). The function of the therapist is to proceed at the client's pace and with the client's unique way of experiencing the world – from the client's idiosyncratic, subjective, perceptual perspective.

At the root of this approach to therapy is the principle that every organism, including the human one, has an actualizing tendency which implies that individuals will seek to 'grow, develop, expand, differentiate, maintain themselves, restore themselves and realize their natures as best they can under their circumstances' (Brodley, 1990, p. 88). It is, therefore, conducive to the client's optimal growth. The therapist exclusively rejects the role of diagnostician or technical expert and instead goes as a companion with the client in the journey of self-exploration and growth. The therapist must have trust in the belief that the client is fundamentally capable of determining his or her own constructive growth. Without such trust, therapy cannot take place (Thorne, 1984).

The person-centred way of producing a therapeutic climate is evidenced in the way in which the client is seen as fundamentally trustworthy and valued. It is demonstrated through the practice of the 'core conditions' which are the basic tenets of the Rogerian viewpoint. When Rogers wrote about the 'necessary and sufficient conditions for therapeutic personality change' (Rogers, 1957) he listed six criteria which, effectively, can be distilled into what have commonly become known as the three core conditions – empathy, unconditional positive regard, and congruence. He suggested that an individual would change (in terms of overall personality) 'at both surface and deeper levels, in a direction in which clinicians would agree means greater integration, less internal conflict, more energy utilizable for effective living' (Rogers, 1957, p. 95). A number of writers have raised objections to the view of the sufficiency and necessity of these conditions (Truax and Carkhuff, 1967; Thorne, 1984; Cramer, 1990), though the person-centred approach largely retains the position postulated by Rogers.

The first condition, empathy, was explicated by Rogers thus: 'to sense the client's private world as if it were your own, but without ever losing the "as if" quality' (Rogers, 1957, p. 99). Patterson (1980) suggests that while congruence or unconditional positive regard may at times be the most significant position, empathy has the highest priority. Empathy refers to the therapist's attempt to enter the client's world and become thoroughly conversant with it (Thorne, 1984). It has been suggested by a number of writers (Thorne, 1984; Mearns and Thorne, 1988) that even when empathic listening is inexact or unsuccessful, it is still valuable, as the very attempt to be in tune with another person is of itself important and helpful to the therapeutic relationship. Empathy is a rare quality but is perhaps the most trainable of the three core conditions. It can also be the most powerful of them all in terms of creative change for the client (Thorne, 1984).

A number of critics of the Rogerian approach have linked empathy with the therapist's behaviour of reflection or simply repeating back to the client the last few words of his or her statement. Bozarth (1984) asserts that reflection is merely a technique, a behavioural device by which the therapist reports back to the client, whereas empathy is in reality an ongoing process. Though various attempts have been made to quantify empathy (Barrett-Lennard, 1962; Truax and Carkhuff, 1967; Carkhuff, 1971), Bozarth (1984) believes that such an approach reinforces a skills-training-model view of counselling and has altered and restricted the original meaning of the construct. Mearns (1984) has suggested that empathy is the ability to understand how the client feels in his or her world, which in turn helps the client take responsibility for his or her feelings and even permits the search and exploration of deeper understandings. It is perhaps the communication of this empathic feeling and understanding which is central to the process of enabling the client to feel understood. In this way, empathy will have its greatest impact.

Rogers (1959) stated that empathy is the state of perceiving the internal frame of reference of another with accuracy and with the emotional components and meanings which pertain thereto, as if one were the other person, but without ever losing the 'as if', condition. It is perhaps this process of getting as close as possible to another person's perception of reality, or construct system, that often becomes very difficult for the therapist. Attempting to actually perceive the harsh reality of the world through the lens of another person can cause enormous difficulty, especially when one is still attempting to hold on to one's own (i.e. the therapist's) reality. True empathic understanding often takes time to develop, and Thorne (1984) spoke to the importance of therapists feeling secure or 'anchored' in their own identity in order to express empathy. It is, therefore, of primary importance for the therapist to remain 'anchored' as such a process will be necessary for both client and therapist as they work towards positive growth in the client's self-concept.

The second basic condition is unconditional positive regard. Synonyms that have been put forward include acceptance, non-possessive love, liking, caring and warmth. Rogers states boldly that this condition can be summarized thus: 'to the extent that the therapist finds himself experiencing a warm acceptance of each aspect of a client's experience as being a part of that client, he is experiencing unconditional positive regard' (Rogers, 1957, p. 98) (though he does emphasize in a footnote that complete acceptance can only be achieved theoretically or at best fleetingly). Mearns (1985) has pointed to the possibility of this condition being seen in a cold clinical light when in fact the very opposite is intended. Thorne (1984) has even suggested that this area may be seen as the most important of all by the client on first entering therapy. Often clients will be coming to therapy situations from a background of treatment by others which has emphasized the very opposite of the total acceptance that the therapist attempts to convey. The client may have been the recipient of harsh judgemental attitudes and of acceptance which has been conditional on the production of requisite behaviours. 'I will love and accept you if you behave the way I would like you to' may well have been the background from which the client has been socialized. He or she may accordingly expect to find, and perhaps be surprised to encounter the absence of, such conditions being put on their worth.

Rogers (1959) used the word 'prizing', borrowed from the philosopher John Dewey, which implies an acceptance of the client in a non-selective or evaluating way and involves as much acceptance of the client's 'bad' (i.e. negative) feelings as of the 'good' (i.e. positive, mature and confident) ones. Consequently, even though it may not be an easy step to take initially, the therapist should be able to accept the client without seeking to approve of his or her behaviour, accepting that this is the client's reality at this time and accepting the client as a person of worth. Mearns (1985) has shown how clients can easily erect a pattern of circular defensive reactions which reifies the belief that because they feel unloved they begin to act in a defensive way which then acts as a shield that keeps other people away. It is by offering an enduring acceptance that the therapist is in a position to enable the client to break out of this vicious circle. Of course, it is not just the therapist feeling warm or accepting towards the client which is the crux of the matter; rather it is the communication of this feeling to the client so that the client can perceive this acceptance that is of essential importance.

Lietaer (1984) suggested that it is possible to split this component into three distinguishable sections – positive regard, non-directivity, and unconditionality. He argues that Rogers did not really go into great detail about this condition. He (Lietaer) also discusses the obvious difficulty of total unconditionality, which he sees as being impossible to achieve. However, it is the very attempt by the therapist to go with the client at the time of the encounter that is important. To do this the therapist does not have to suspend her or his own belief system but needs to convey acceptance of the client's system as being meaningful to the client at this particular time. As such, the therapist does not seek to approve the client's behaviour but seeks to understand and accept it as being something here and now for the client (Lietaer, 1984). Mearns (1985) has clarified this position by making it clear that the therapist is not responsible for the client's behaviour but is responsible to the client. In this way there is less chance that the therapist will be perceived as being a guarantor of any successful outcome.

The third basic condition is congruence, which is sometimes termed genuineness, realness, authenticity or harmony. Mearns and Thorne (1988) distinguish the three conditions by defining empathy as a process, unconditional positive regard as an attitude, and congruence as a 'state of being'. In this way it is perhaps easy to see how this latter condition may be regarded as the essential humanness of the therapist. Patterson (1980), also referring to it as a state of being, sees congruence as being self-experiences which are accurately symbolized in the self-concept and speaks of the therapist as being integrated, genuine and whole. Watson (1984) sees congruence as a precondition for the therapist's experience of the other two core conditions – empathy and acceptance. It appears that is not something that can be acquired through reading; it has to be established by the therapist being able to value the client in his or her individuality but also by the client accepting him/herself, which in turn also implies trusting on the part of the therapist. Without this the therapist becomes a sort of reactive actor – putting on a performance for and with the client where the genuine responses are, for whatever reasons, edited and altered or even distorted to fit the situation as perceived to be appropriate by the therapist. Being genuine is not synonymous with self-disclosure in that the relevance of a therapist's feeling to the therapeutic session may not be high. It may be totally inappropriate for the therapist to simply express feelings that she or he genuinely feels at any one moment, as the timing or even importance to the client may not be germane.

Mearns (1986) has suggested that congruence might be seen as the most threatening of the core conditions, particularly for professionals who may be used to dealing with well-rehearsed techniques and therefore may feel uncomfortable behaving in such an open and honest way with clients. Truax and Carkhuff (1967) put this issue of whether or not congruence is important by asking the question: 'How can we expect authenticity in our clients if we as counsellors are not authentic in therapy?' Thus congruence implies transparency and lack of pretence as well as absence of any professional front or exterior behind which the therapist might attempt to hide when the situation in the therapeutic encounter becomes difficult.

STRESS MANAGEMENT AND THE PERSON-CENTRED THERAPIST

Over the past few years the increasing awareness of stress – in its many forms – has resulted in the growth of a veritable industry to provide remedial help. A whole range of interdisciplinary approaches to the topic has resulted, but as yet no clear or rigorous definition of the term or its aetiology has appeared (Sutherland and Cooper, 1990). A variety of models – engineering, medical, psychological – have been presented in an effort to understand what is becoming a major cause for concern at both the personal and the institutional level (Dutch *et al.*, 1993). The question that is usually posed relates to the aetiology of personal dysfunction and has inherent biomedical overtones (Barnard, 1984).

To the person-centred therapist, the question that is asked is a rather different one. She or he (the therapist) would be more concerned with the client's personal and subjective attributions of any perceived 'problem'. In such a way, the individual's phenomenological construct system is given pride of place in any work which may be carried out between therapist and client. As a result of taking such a position, a nosology of stressors becomes irrelevant. This is not to suggest that the individual person-centred therapist is a conforming robot constrained by the boundaries of Rogerian theory; rather it places the client at the focal point of the therapeutic dialogue. There are a number of ways in which person-centred therapists have been eclectic in their own practice (Lietaer, 1990) but the difference between the person-centred approach and other forms of therapeutic intervention lies in the way the therapist works within the therapeutic encounter, particularly in terms of her or his rejection of an expert position and positive acceptance of the client's subjective view of reality.

Rogers developed a theory of personality which evolved from his experiences as a therapist and placed great emphasis on the notion of the self. His theory is basically a phenomenological one in that it emphasizes the client's experiences of reality: 'the best vantage point of understanding behaviour is from the internal frame of reference of the individual' (Rogers, 1951, p. 494). At the core of his personality theory is the belief that the growth in the concept of the self results from an interaction between the organismic or real self and the self-construct, which occurs through a gradual evaluation of the individual through contact with others. This 'dawning of the I experience' (Rogers, 1951, p. 498) is often produced by the introjection of attitudes from significant others which are in conflict with the values that youngsters attach to experiences of organic functioning. Thus, a distorted symbolization of experience develops, so that the person becomes distrustful of the organismic self. However, as the need for positive regard and approval from others is strong, conflict arises, so that the individual begins to develop a self-construct that is divorced from his or her own innate resources (Mearns and Thorne, 1988). This search for outside approval and guidance results in what Rogers terms a 'locus of evaluation' which is externally oriented. It sees the values expressed by outside forces such as parents, friends, even therapist, as more important than the individual's own organismic feelings. In contrast, the fully functioning person would have a locus of evaluation that is largely rooted internally. It is the role of the therapist to attempt to change the client's external locus of evaluation into a more internalized one in which the organismic self is more closely in tune with the self-concept.

Stressed clients – those that are experiencing some perceived disturbance or difficulty in their life with which they feel they cannot cope – may well be suffering from some imbalance between their organismic self and their self-concept. Rogers (1951, pp. 526–7) describes diagrammatically how such a personality, which is in a state of psychological tension, may differ from that of a fully functioning being. Though he points out that there may well be a whole number of elements of experience which the client is perceiving, not all will necessarily be causing conflict.

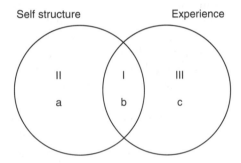

Figure 3.1 *Personality in state of psychological disturbance*

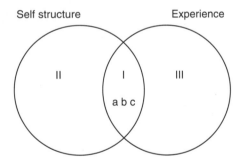

Figure 3.2 *Personality after successful therapy*

An example of how one stressor might be perceived by a client may prove instructive. Figures 3.1 and 3.2 each comprise two circles:

Self-structure This represents the configuration of concepts which make up the structure of the self or the concept of the self. It includes 'the patterned perceptions of an individual's characteristics and relationships, together with the values associated with these. It is available to awareness' (Rogers, 1951, p. 525).

Experience This represents the immediate field of a person's experiences from all sensory modalities. It is fluid. These experiences cover three areas:

Area I   In this part of a person's phenomenal field, the concept of self and self-in-relationship is congruent with the evidence perceived through sensory and visceral experience.

Area II   This is the part of a person's phenomenal field in which environmental experiences (of people or events) have been distorted in symbolization and become perceived as part of a person's own experience. For example, attitudes and values from parents or significant others are introjected by an individual and perceived phenomenologically as being the product of sensory evidence.

Area III   This part is composed of those sensory and visceral experiences which are denied to awareness because they are inconsistent with the concept of the self.

If a male client, for example, expressed the view that he was experiencing some form of work-related stress, this might be seen in terms of the Rogerian diagrammatic outline. In terms of Figure 3.1, representing a personality in a state of psychological disturbance, experience (a) represents the view that the client feels inadequate in dealing with the pressures of his job, experience (b) would be the client's experience of failure at his job, and experience (c) relates to the position where the client is successful at this job. This latter is obviously inconsistent with the concept of the self and so cannot be admitted directly into awareness. Though impossible to deny completely, it becomes distorted so that any threat to the structure of the self is eliminated. It might appear to the consciousness in ways which suggest that the individual is fortunate or undeserving. Such a distortion could fit into Area II in the diagram since it is consistent with the self-concept, but the actual experience itself is denied in any symbolized form and remains in Area III.

In terms of Figure 3.2, representing a personality after successful therapy, the areas remain the same but the relationship between them now changes. In terms of experience (a), the client might realize that people think he is not able to handle the pressures of the job but recognize that they are not always correct. Experience (b) would be evidenced when the client actually feels this at work; experience (c) could be the client's view that he has a number of other skills that enable him to cope with the demands of his job. In this way, experience (a) no longer is perceived in a distorted fashion but rather as sensory evidence of the attitudes of others, while experience (c) is admitted into awareness and organized into the self-structure.

Thus the goal of integrated personality developed is the fostering of congruence between the phenomenal field of experience and the conceptual structure of the self. If such congruence is attained, it will mean 'freedom from internal strain and anxiety' (Rogers, 1951, p. 532). Consequently, the person-centred therapist working with clients who are in a state of stress would be aware of the position wherein some individuals might be more vulnerable to stressors due to the client's locus of evaluation being external rather than internal. It is a prime function of the therapist to redress this balance so that the locus of evaluation shifts towards the client. Then the client's perceptions of events, and consequently their ability to deal with them from their own innate resources, are enhanced.

As notions of health become more holistic in orientation, mere absence of disease has been replaced by ideas of positive and active health. The dated medical model, which emphasized the view that remedying all dysfunctions was dependent on the exact determination of some pathology (Fruggeri, 1992), has given way to the recognition that the individual's perception of his or her phenomenological world could well be connected to his or her physical as well as mental health. Thus the dichotomy between physical and mental health has been replaced with a more balanced, holistic view of the person. Various writers have alluded to the importance of the individual's phenomenological reality in understanding stress: for example, Lazarus (1966), Cox (1985) and Cooper *et al.* (1988, p. 11) see stress as 'a misfit between an individual and his particular environment'. In this way, a person's idiosyncratic reaction to a seemingly common stressor might be better understood. It supports the position that the best way of dealing with stress in terms of a therapeutic encounter is to engage clients on the basis of their own reality and from their own frame of reference.

This 'assumption of the individual knower' (McNamee and Gergen, 1992) resonates throughout a number of theoretical approaches to therapy (experiential, personal construct, social construction, hermeneutics). Such approaches place great emphasis on the individual's construction of reality and reject the traditional view of therapist as scientist. Equally, the expert position of the therapist which reifies client–therapist separation is replaced by a more mutual and equitable encounter between them. In terms of precise person-centred therapy, the issues that the client then brings to the therapeutic hour are of total importance and determine how the therapist behaves towards the client. The presenting problem might be seemingly innocuous in normative terms but from the individual client's attributional framework it might be interpreted quite differently.

Rogers (1957) gives the example of how a student's fear of an examination at the organismic level may lead to a more generalized fear of the university or examination room. This results because of the incongruence between the organismic self and self-structure – i.e. the discrepancy between the way the examination registers in the student's organism, and the symbolic representation of that experience in awareness so that it does conflict with the view the student has of him/herself. For another student exhibiting similar symptoms, a quite different reaction might take place. Another example of idiosyncratic attributions comes from Anderson and Goolishian in a case study of a client who believed he had a contagious disease when, in fact, no 'scientific' evidence of any pathology was found (Anderson and Goolishian, 1992, pp. 34–6). In this case it was only the therapist dealing directly with the client's perceptual phenomena which enabled some movement to take place.

Thus dealing with any stressor that might be experienced by the client must be done from the client's framework. Fruggeri (1992) believes that in dealing with dysfunctional issues it is not so much the aetiology of symptoms which is the core issue but rather the interpersonal and social processes that maintain these symptoms. Consequently, the person-centred approach would be more concerned with the client's subjective appreciation of his or her own dysfunctions in so far as they prevent his or her optimal growth. Any issue which might then be regarded as stressful to that client can be addressed from his or her standpoint, with the therapist in support. This position is stated most clearly by Mearns and McLeod (1984) when pointing out that the philosophy of the person-centred approach is not a series of specific technical competencies but a general framework for understanding persons.

Such a position is in marked contrast to many of the approaches currently offered by practitioners who engage in a skills-based approach (see Chapters 4, 5 and 6). The literature is replete with myriad strategies and techniques for managing stress (Davis *et al.*, 1988). Though a complete list of these would be beyond the scope of this chapter, it is fair to say that many of these approaches come from the behavioural sciences and include cognitive as well as behavioural items such as visualization, self-hypnosis, cognitive restructuring, attention control training, visuo-motor behaviour rehearsal, biofeedback and stress inoculation training.

Such categorizations are not of prime importance to the person-centred therapist. The central issue would be the extent to which the therapeutic conversation (Anderson and Goolishian, 1992) could give the client enough space to feel sufficiently competent to make a decision about how particular techniques might be of help to him or her. For the therapist to make such decisions would be counter to the basic tenets implicit in the person-centred approach. It could pre-empt or sidetrack the client's locus of evaluation and make him or her more vulnerable to external forces. Further, it would emphasize the therapist's view of the world as the correct, expert one, whereas the main objective of the person-centred therapist would be to develop the client's own awareness of his or her (the client's) judgement about what is right for him or her.

Thus, the person-centred therapist would be mostly concerned with the client's perceived meaning of the stresses which were being experienced, rather than offering some quick, cook-book recipe or mechanical intervention. This is not to deny that many individuals do benefit from some directive interventions. Such techniques or strategies, however, would be seen by the person-centred therapist as treating the client at a superficial level and not attending to the more fundamental meaning of any stresses to the client's overall self-concept. It is with enhancing this more crucial aspect of an individual that the person-centred therapist would be most concerned.

CONCLUSION

An individual who voluntarily enters into a dialogue with a therapist is implicitly in some form of stress. An analysis or classification of the exact nature and aetiology of the dysfunction is not the prime concern of the person-centred therapist: what is more crucially relevant is the establishment of a therapeutic climate which will be perceived by the client as being rewarding for him or her. Rogers expressly believed that the use of the three core conditions of empathy, acceptance and genuineness on the part of the therapist were not only necessary but sufficient to promote the development of the actualizing tendency. Reliance on technical expertise is eschewed: in its place, the therapist offers a trusting relationship of equality with the client. In such a way, no matter how damaged the client's self-concept might be, no matter what is the nature of the stressor, the client is seen as capable, through his/her own inherent actualizing capability, of developing as a person. Thus the person-centred therapist is not likely to offer ready-made, magical cures or to direct the client towards following any particular coping strategy. Rather, by offering a trusting relationship in which the client is valued as a person, issues which are disabling to the client can be overcome. It is the client who has the ability to help him/herself, and he or she does this by walking a path with the therapist as a valued companion along the way. It is by utilizing the individual's attributional system that the therapist is able to go where the client instinctively feels capable of going, at the client's behest and at his or her pace, and it is this that results in therapeutic change.

Stress is thus seen by the person-centred therapist in a much broader way than mere temporary upset to the individual. Barnard (1984) reveals how the individual's perception of distress can have far-reaching effects. Utilizing the position adopted by Cassell (1979), he distinguishes between disease (the physical and chemical process that disrupts organic function) and the illness (the personal experience of disease). Such an approach makes it evident how stress-induced illness might be seen as 'challenges to the sense of identity and meaning that often accompany physical distress' (Barnard, 1984). It is really these challenges to self-identity that the person-centred therapist is dedicated to meeting by harnessing the client's unique resources for self-healing.

REFERENCES

Anderson, H. and Goolishian, H. (1992) The client is the expert: A not-knowing approach to therapy. In S. McNamee and K. Gergen (eds), *Therapy as Social Construction*, pp. 25–39, London: Sage.

Barnard, D. (1984) The personal meaning of illness: Client centred dimension of medicine and health care. In R.E. Levant and J.M. Shlien (eds), *Client Centered Therapy and the Person Centered Approach: New Directions in Theory, Research and Practice*, pp. 337–51. New York: Praeger.

Barrett-Lennard, G.T. (1962) Dimensions of therapist response as causal factors in therapeutic change. *Psychological Monographs*, **76**:43, whole no. 562.

Bozarth, J.D. (1984) Beyond reflection: Emergent modes of empathy. In R.F. Levant and J.M. Shlien (eds), *Client Centered Therapy and the Person Centered Approach: New Directions in Theory, Research and Practice*, pp. 59–75. New York: Praeger.

Brodley, B.T. (1990) Client centered and experiential: Two different therapies. In G. Lietaer, J. Rombauts and R. Van Balen (eds), *Client Centered and Experiential Psychotherapy in the Nineties*, pp. 87–105. Louvain: Louvain University Press.

Carkhuff, R.R. (1971) *The Development of Human Resources*. New York: Holt, Rinehart & Winston.

Cassell, E.J. (1979) *The Healer's Art: A New Approach to the Doctor–Patient Relationship*. Baltimore: Penguin.

Cooper, C.L., Cooper, R.D. and Eaker, L.H. (1988) *Living with Stress.* Harmondsworth: Penguin.

Cox, T. (1985) The nature and measurement of stress. *Ergonomics*, **28**, 1155–63.

Cramer, D. (1990) The necessary conditions for evaluating client centered therapy. In G. Lietaer, J. Rombauts and R. Van Balen (eds), *Client Centered and Experiential Psychotherapy in the Nineties*, pp. 415–28. Louvain: Louvain University Press.

Davis, M., Eshelman, E.R. and McKay, M. (1988) *The Relaxation and Stress Reduction Handbook* (3rd edn) Oakland: New Harbinger.

Dutch, R., Clarke, P.T. and Christie, D. (1993) *Stress in Lecturers in Colleges of Education in Scotland.* Report commissioned by the Educational Institute of Scotland Association of Lecturers in Colleges of Education in Scotland.

Fruggeri, L. (1992) Therapeutic process as the social construction of change. In S. McNamee and K.J. Gergen (eds), *Therapy as Social Construction*, pp. 40–53. London: Sage.

Lazarus, R.S. (1966) *Psychological Stress and the Coping Process.* New York: McGraw-Hill.

Lietaer, G. (1984) Unconditional positive regard: A controversial basic attitude in client centered therapy. In R.F. Levant and J.M. Shlien (eds), *Client Centered Therapy and the Person Centered Approach: New Directions in Theory, Research and Practice*, pp. 41–58. New York: Praeger.

Lietaer, G. (1990) The client centered approach after the Wisconsin project: A personal view on its evaluation. In G. Lietaer, J. Rombauts and R. Van Balen (eds), *Client Centered and Experiential Psychotherapy in the Nineties*, pp. 19–45. Louvain: Louvain University Press.

McNamee, S. and Gergen, K.J. (1992) *Therapy as Social Construction.* London: Sage.

Mearns, D. (1984) Some notes on empathy. Jordanhill College, Glasgow.

Mearns, D. (1985) Some notes on unconditional positive regard. Jordanhill College, Glasgow.

Mearns, D. (1986) Some notes on congruence: Can I dare to be me in response to my client? Unpublished paper presented to the first Facilitator Development Institute (Britain) training course.

Mearns, D. and McLeod, J. (1984) A person centered approach to research. In R.F. Levant and J.M. Shlien (eds), *Client Centered Therapy and the Person Centered Approach: New Directions in Theory, Research and Practice*, pp. 370–89. New York: Praeger.

Mearns, D. and Thorne, B. (1988) *Person Centred Counselling in Action.* London: Sage.

Patterson, C.H. (1980) *Theories of Counseling and Psychotherapy* (3rd edn). New York: Harper & Row.

Rogers, C.R. (1951) *Client-Centred Therapy.* London: Constable.

Rogers, C.R. (1957) The necessary and sufficient conditions of therapeutic personality change. *Journal of Consulting Psychology*, **21**, 95–103.

Rogers, C.R. (1959) A theory of personality and interpersonal relationships as developed in the person centered framework. In S. Koch (ed.), *Psychology: A Study of a Science*, Vol. 3, pp. 184–256. New York: McGraw-Hill.

Sutherland, V.J. and Cooper, C.L. (1990) *Understanding Stress: A Psychological Perspective for Health Professionals*. London: Chapman & Hall.

Thorne, B. (1984) Person-centred therapy. In W. Dryden (ed.), *Individual Therapy in Britain*, pp. 102–8. London: Harper & Row.

Truax, C.B. and Carkhuff, R.R. (1967) *Toward Effective Counseling and Psychotherapy*. Chicago: Aldine.

Watson, N. (1984) The empirical status of Rogers's hypothesis of the necessary and sufficient conditions for effective psychotherapy. In R.F. Levant and J.M. Shlien (eds), *Client Centered Therapy and the Person Centered Approach: New Directions in Theory, Research and Practice*, pp. 17–40. New York: Praeger.

CHAPTER 4

The Multimodal Approach: Theory, Assessment, Techniques and Interventions

Stephen Palmer

Multimodal therapy is a systematic, technically eclectic approach which has been adapted to the field of stress counselling and stress management. It has been used in a variety of contexts including clinical and industrial settings. Arnold Lazarus (1981; 1989), the originator of multimodal therapy, contends that the entire range of personality can be covered within seven specific modalities: Behaviour, Affect, Sensation, Imagery, Cognition, Interpersonal, and Drugs/Biology. A stress client's modalities are systematically assessed and an individual stress counselling or training programme is then formulated. This chapter focuses on the theory and practice of multimodal therapy applied to the field of stress counselling and management and discusses the multimodal-transactional model of stress.

INTRODUCTION: WHY USE THE MULTIMODAL APPROACH?

Karasu (1986) estimated that there were at least 400 'schools' of psychotherapy. London (1964, p. 33) noted that 'however interesting, plausible and appealing a theory may be, it is techniques, not theories, that are actually used on people. Study of the effects of psychotherapy, therefore is always the study of the effectiveness of techniques.' If each 'school' of psychotherapy has its own basic techniques and assuming that Karasu and London are correct, a therapist adhering to eclecticism could use literally hundreds of different techniques. However, the number is reduced if the different approaches use similar techniques.

A problem may arise when choosing suitable techniques or interventions for use with a specific problem. Palmer and Dryden (1991, p. 3) stated, with reference to stress management training and psychotherapy, 'from the array of techniques that can be taught within a psychoeducational framework, it is possible that the trainer/therapist may not choose or suggest the most appropriate techniques that would be in the client's best interest'. Lazarus (1990) asserted that 'unsystematic eclecticism is practised by therapists who require neither a coherent rationale nor empirical validation for the methods they employ. This is in contrast to systematic prescriptive (technical) eclectics who base their endeavours on data from the four-fold impact of the therapeutic alliance, client qualities, clinical skills and specific techniques.' Norcross and Grencavage (1990, p. 10) believe that 'the common thread is that technical eclecticism is relatively atheoretical, pragmatic, and empirical'. The technical eclectic does not necessarily apply the meta-belief systems of the different 'schools' of psychotherapy.

During the 1960s and 1970s, Lazarus developed multimodal therapy which advocates technical eclecticism. Some of the most useful aspects of multimodal therapy in its application to stress management, counselling and psychotherapy are 'its comprehensive, yet straightforward assessment procedures, which aid a trainer/therapist to develop and negotiate with a client an individual programme' (Palmer and Dryden, 1991, p. 3). The fundamental premise is that 'clients are usually troubled by a multitude of specific problems that should be dealt with by a similar multitude of specific treatments … the multimodal approach stresses that all therapy needs to be tailored to the individual requirements of each person and situation' (Lazarus, 1981, cover). The therapy is flexible enough to be tailored to fit the individual needs of the client, rather than the client needing to fit the therapy or its belief system. Interestingly Maslow's comment that if you only have a hammer you treat everything like a nail is probably nearer the truth than can be imagined. (Norcross and Grencavage (1990, p. 21) believe that the 'history of psychotherapy has repeatedly confirmed this observation'.) The practice of multimodal therapy should overcome this problem. Although Beitman (1990, p. 65) criticized multimodal therapy, he believed that 'counsellors must build flexibility into their approaches to their clients. This flexibility may be imagined as the counsellor's moulding around the other, a fitting with the client rather than forcing the patient into the therapist's own theoretical bed.'

Lazarus (1990, p. 34) believes that many therapists 'overlooked the false conclusions of meta-analysis and contend that all treatment outcomes are similar'. This was in relation to the widely cited work of Smith *et al.* (1980) which in fact, did find in 'well controlled' studies that behaviour therapy was superior to psychodynamic and other verbal therapies. Lazarus (1990, p. 34) alleges that 'to ignore technique specificity is a serious breach of professional responsibility as specific treatments can be recommended for specific problems'. Examples of technique specificity would be response prevention for obsessive compulsive disorders (see Grayson *et al.*, 1985) and exposure for phobics (Marks, 1987).

Multimodal therapy (Lazarus, 1981) goes further than just applying a collection of techniques. It 'operates within a consistent theoretical base, and endeavours to pinpoint various processes and principles' (Lazarus, 1990, p. 40). The multimodal framework is underpinned by general systems theory, social learning theory (Bandura, 1986), and group and communications theory (Lazarus, 1987). Multimodal stress counselling and stress management is also underpinned by an adapted version of the transactional model of stress (see Palmer and Dryden, 1995).

This chapter includes a section on the multimodal-transactional model of stress and illustrates the comprehensive assessment and treatment procedures of multimodal therapy as applied to counselling, psychotherapy and stress management.

MODALITIES

Lazarus believes that the entire range of personality can be covered within seven specific modalities (Lazarus, 1981; 1989). This helps the therapist achieve a (w)holistic understanding of an individual. The seven modalities are:

Behaviour
Affect
Sensation
Imagery
Cognition
Interpersonal
Drugs/Biology

This blueprint is known by the acronym BASIC I.D. and is used for the assessment of clients.

MULTIMODAL-TRANSACTIONAL MODEL OF STRESS

The working model of stress used by Palmer and Dryden (see *Counselling for Stress Problems*, 1995) adapted for stress counselling is known as 'transactional'. This model provides a simple but realistic explanation of the complicated nature of stress as it addresses the interrelationship between the internal and the external world of individuals. Palmer and Dryden (1995) modified the transactional models of stress proposed by Cox (1978) and Cox and Mackay (1981) to incorporate Lazarus's seven modalities. Figure 4.1 illustrates the new multimodal-transactional model.

In the model, the psychological processes are of fundamental importance. How a person reacts to an event is more due to his or her perceptions of it and his or her perceived abilities to deal with it than to the event or situation itself. Therefore the event can be considered as a potential 'trigger' to activate stress response but not necessarily the main cause of its activation. Once the event has passed, the person may remain disturbed about it due to the action or interaction of the different modalities. For example, individuals suffering from a chronic form of stress known as post-traumatic stress disorder may repeatedly see negative images of the event, may have many negative cognitions, may have physiological symptoms of severe anxiety, and may avoid anything that reminds them of the event. This response can still occur years after the stressful event. In other cases, clients who suffer an apparently harmless life-event, such as the death of a pet, become overwhelmed by immense grief, as the event takes on another personal meaning, e.g. anxiety about their own death or memories of the loss of a close family member.

The multimodal-transactional model comprises five discrete stages:

In Stage 1, a pressure is usually perceived by the individual to be emanating from an external source in the environment, e.g. having to meet an important deadline. In fact, there are also day-to-day physiological and psychological needs or demands an individual has in order to survive, such as food and water.

Stage 2 reflects the individual's perception of the pressure or demand and her

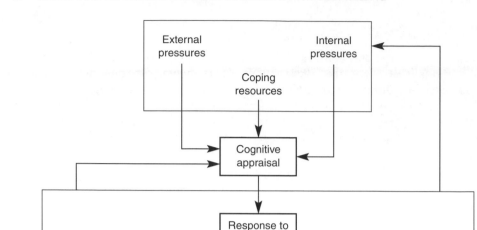

Figure 4.1 *Multimodal-transactional model of stress*
Source: Palmer and Dryden, 1995

appraisal of her ability to deal with it. If the individual perceives that she can cope, even if she is being unrealistic, then she may stay in the situation, e.g. working towards a deadline. If it happens that the person perceives that she cannot cope, then at that moment she may experience stress. However, added to this equation are social, family or cultural beliefs which the individual may have subsumed into her belief system. Thus, if the individual believes that she 'must' always perform well at work, an innocuous deadline may assume great importance. In reality, the 'must' is an internal and not an external pressure as the individual does not have to hold rigidly on to this belief. Many clients receiving stress counselling cognitively appraise experiences as 'very stressful' as a result of their beliefs which distort the importance of an actual or feared event. In this stage, then, the individual decides whether she has the resources to cope with the external and internal pressures of a specific situation. If she believes that she can deal with the situation then her stress response is less likely to be activated. However, if she perceives that she does not have the coping strategies to deal with the situation then she progresses on to Stage 3 of the model.

In Stage 3, psychophysiological changes occur. Taken together, these comprise what is generally known as the 'stress response'. There is usually an emotion or combination of emotions such as anxiety, anger or guilt. According to our multimodal-transactional model, these emotions may have behavioural, sensory, imaginal, cognitive, interpersonal and biological/physiological components (see Figure 4.1). In addition, there will probably be behavioural and cognitive attempts to change the environment or escape from the situation and thereby reduce the pressure. However, like animals, some individuals have been known to freeze with fear, which is not always helpful.

Stage 4 relates to the consequences of the application of the coping strategies or responses of the individual. Once again, the individual's perception of the coping strategies applied is important. Consequently, if an individual believes that his intervention is not helping, he may picture himself as failing which, in itself, becomes an additional strain in the situation. Actual failure to meet the demand is also detrimental if the individual truly believes that the demand has to be met in a satisfactory manner.

Stage 5 is concerned with the feedback system. Interventions may be made by the individual which may reduce or alter the external or internal pressures. If this occurs then the organism may return to a neutral state of equilibrium. However, if the interventions are ineffective, then the individual may experience prolonged stress. This has many psychophysiological consequences which may even lead to mental breakdown or death in extreme cases. Death may be due to the prolonged effect of the stress hormones – adrenaline, noradrenaline and cortisol – on the body.

Individuals who have managed to cope with difficult life events may view themselves as possessing coping skills which they can apply in similar situations. This is known as 'self-efficacy' and is a major cognitive component in the appraisal of future events as non-threatening and therefore not stressful. They may hold beliefs such as: '*I'm in control.*' '*I know I can do it.*' '*This will not be a problem.*' '*This will be a challenge and not stressful.*' These beliefs often prevent the person from going beyond Stage 2 of our multimodal-transactional model. Coping is considered by researchers (e.g. Dewe *et al.*, 1993; Lazarus, R.S. 1966; Lazarus, R.S. and Folkman, 1984) as an 'important part of the overall stress process' (Cox, 1993, p. 20) and, whenever possible, multimodal stress counselling attempts to help clients improve their coping strategies.

Multimodal stress counsellors and stress management trainers teach clients how to intervene at the most appropriate stage of the multimodal-transactional model. Whenever possible, clients are shown how to improve their coping resources and how to moderate their appraisal of difficult situations (see 'Tracking', p. 54). However, clients suffering from burnout are likely to be in Stage 5 of the model and require a comprehensive programme of treatment. This requires a thorough therapeutic assessment to ensure that the most suitable interventions are selected.

THERAPEUTIC ASSESSMENT

The initial interview is used to derive 13 determinations (adapted from Lazarus, 1989; Palmer and Dryden, 1995 p. 19).

1. Are there signs of 'psychosis'?
2. Are there signs of organicity, organic pathology or any disturbed motor activity?
3. Is there evidence of depression,or suicidal or homicidal tendencies?
4. What are the persisting complaints and their main precipitating events?
5. What appear to be some important antecedent factors?
6. Who or what seems to be maintaining the client's overt and covert problems?
7. What does the client wish to derive from counselling, therapy or training?
8. Are there clear indications or contra-indications for the adoption of a particular therapeutic style?
9. Are there any indications as to whether it would be in the client's best interests to be seen individually, as part of a dyad, triad, family unit and/or in a group?
10. Can a mutually satisfying relationship ensue, or should the client be referred elsewhere?
11. Has the client previous experience of counselling, therapy or relevant training? If yes, what was the outcome?
12. Why is the client seeking therapy at this time and why not last week, last month or last year?
13. What are some of the client's positive attributes and strengths?

To investigate the modalities and problem identifications in further depth, at the end of the initial interview the client is asked to complete a 15–page 'multimodal life history inventory' at home (Lazarus and Lazarus, 1991). In addition, the MLHI looks at the client's expectations of therapy including what personal qualities they think the

Table 4.1 *Modality profile (or BASIC I.D. chart)*

Behaviour	Avoidance of social events
	Avoidance of public transport
	Sleep disturbances
Affect	Anger and irritability
	Anxiety attacks
	Guilt
Sensation	Tension
Imagery	Images of physical abuse
	Frequent nightmares
Cognition	Must perform well
	Life should not be unfair
	Self-downing statements
	Low frustration statements, e.g. 'I can't stand it.'
Interpersonal	Passive/aggressive in relationships
	Few close friends of long standing
Drugs/Biology	Smokes ten cigarettes daily
	Lack of exercise
	Aspirin for headaches
	Unhealthy diet

Table 4.2 *Modality profile (or BASIC I.D. chart) and treatment strategies*

Behaviour	Avoidance of social events	Exposure programme and cognitive restructuring
	Avoidance of public transport	Exposure programme
	Sleep disturbances	Self-hypnosis tape or Benson relaxation response
Affect	Anger and irritability	Anger management/ calming self-statements
	Anxiety attacks	Breathing exercises
	Guilt	Dispute irrational beliefs
Sensation	Tension	Biofeedback/relaxation training (or massage)
Imagery	Images of physical abuse	Imaginal exposure
	Frequent nightmares	Mastery imagery intervention
Cognition	Must perform well	Cognitive restructuring and disputing irrational beliefs
	Life should not be unfair	
	Self-downing statements	
	Low frustration statements, e.g. 'I can't stand it.'	
Interpersonal	Passive/aggressive in relationships	Assertion training
	Few close friends of long standing	Friendship training
Drugs/Biology	Smokes ten cigarettes daily	Behavioural stop smoking programme self-hypnosis
	Lack of exercise	Fitness programme
	Aspirin for headaches	Relaxation training
	Unhealthy diet	Nutrition programme

ideal therapist should possess. This enables the therapist to match, if necessary, their approach to the expectations of the client, e.g. being directive as opposed to being non-directive. Others may want a 'tough, no-nonsense' approach and would find a 'warm, gentle' approach not helpful which could lead to a client dropping out in the early stages of therapy. One client expected the ideal therapist to possess 'objectivity, experience, extensive knowledge and honesty'. This client also thought that therapy was about 'helping me to overcome my problems and feel happier'.

Information obtained from the initial interview and the MLHI helps the therapist to produce a 'comprehensive modality profile'. An example is seen on Table 4.1. This consists of a modality analysis of identified problems. Many adults are capable of writing up their own modality profile if they are given an instruction sheet explaining each modality of the BASIC I.D. The modality profile is the link between assessment and therapy. Each specific problem may need a specific treatment intervention. The problem checklists serve as 'working hypotheses' which may be modified or revised as additional factors come to light (Lazarus, 1987). The modality profile can be completed with the specific treatment strategies noted down (see Table 4.2).

A 'structural profile' is drawn (see Figure 4.2) to elicit more clinical information. This is obtained by asking the client to subjectively rate, on a scale from 1 to 10, how they perceive themselves in relation to the different modalities. This is now usually derived from a part of the MLHI. However, typical questions asked are:

B – How much of a 'doer' are you?
A – How emotional are you?
S – How 'tuned in' are you to your bodily sensations?
I – Do you have a vivid imagination?
C – How much of a thinker are you?
I – How much of a 'social being' are you?
D – Are you health-conscious?

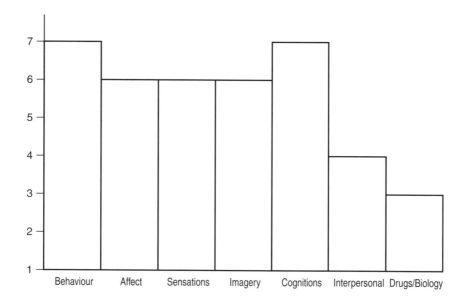

Figure 4.2 *A structural profile*

It can be seen from Figure 4.2 that this client would probably respond well to behavioural tasks/assignments and cognitive restructuring due to the high scores. The structural profile is altered as new information is obtained. It is useful to ask the client in what way they would like to change their profile. The desired structural profile can be drawn (see Figure 4.3). It can be seen that this client wanted to improve her Drugs/Biology modality as she felt this would help her overall physical and mental health.

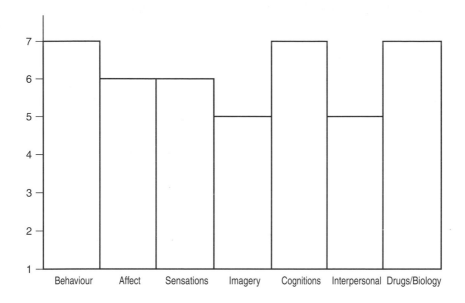

Figure 4.3 *Desired structural profile*

In marital or couples therapy, profiles are compared. It can become apparent that the two individuals may have conflicting profiles which can sometimes negatively affect their relationship, e.g. high and low interpersonal scores.

One of the roles of the therapist is to use their experience and knowledge to indi-cate what particular intervention/techniques may be helpful in tackling a specific problem. In the Behaviour modality in Table 4.2 a number of possible techniques are listed which may help in dealing with sleep disturbances. The client can choose which particular intervention he or she may wish to use. If a client has a strong belief that self-hypnosis would be beneficial then this may be indicated. Meeting client expectancies seems to lead to more positive outcomes (Lazarus, 1973a).

It may be that the multimodal therapist is not sufficiently experienced to teach, for example, self-hypnosis or meditation. Therefore the client would require a refer-ral to another therapist or trainer who was qualified to use these techniques. However, the client would still stay with the primary multimodal therapist to work on the other modalities if necessary.

Individual sessions become task-oriented as the specific problems across the client's BASIC I.D. are covered. The client may decide which particular specific problem they would like to resolve first. However, a glance across the modality profile may indicate that one specific technique could be a useful intervention for problems in different modalities. In Table 4.2 it can be seen that relaxation training may be very appropriate as it appears to be the preferred intervention across three modalities.

The aim is not necessarily to eradicate all of the problems on the modality profile. Large unattainable treatment goals are a hindrance and are to be avoided.

Termination of therapy usually occurs when clients have dealt with the major problems on their modality profile or feel that they can cope with the remaining problems. Some clients do not respond well to a multimodal intervention. Although a BASIC I.D. assessment can still be undertaken, a unimodal or bimodal approach is applied.

SECOND ORDER BASIC I.D.

A second order BASIC I.D. assessment is undertaken when the most obvious techniques have not helped to resolve a problem. The second order assessment concentrates in more detail on the specific problem, as opposed to the initial assessment which looks more at the overview. For example, an individual who tried relaxation training, without success, to cope with panic attacks when speaking publicly may reveal on a close investigation that the cognition '*I must perform well*' triggered her anxiety. Cognitive restructuring and the disputing of the irrational belief would then be preferred intervention.

TRACKING

It is often useful to look at the 'firing order' of the different modalities. A 'late' modality intervention may be unsuccessful. For example, an individual first recognized a bodily sensation of a rapid heart beat, then had the cognitions '*I'm going to have a panic attack. It will be awful. I can't stand it.*' Then he had the image of collapsing in public with a crowd of people looking at him. This would happen within seconds and then he would react behaviourally by escaping from the situation, e.g. getting out of a lift. This was a S–C–I–B sequence (see Table 4.3). If it happened again he was instructed to use momentary relaxation and simultaneously say subvocally '*it's only my heart beat getting faster. It feels bad, but it's not awful. It's not the end of the world. I can stand it.*' If he still had an image of himself collapsing then he would replace this with a pleasant relaxing image. He was instructed not to leave the situation as this would not help him overcome the problem. The 'firing order' of the modalities is matched with a sequence of specific modality interventions. A different 'firing order' would need a different order of interventions. This may explain why relaxation techniques are only effective with some individuals who suffer from panic attacks as the other modalities need to be considered.

BRIDGING

Often a client has a preferred modality which they may use to communicate with the therapist, e.g. talking about the sensation or images they may experience. Bridging is a procedure whereby the therapist may initially 'key into' the client's preferred modality before exploring a modality that the client may avoid, e.g. affect/emotions (see Lazarus, 1987). This is undertaken if it may be clinically useful to examine the avoided modality.

Table 4.3 *Modality 'firing order' sequence*

1. **Sensation** – rapid heartbeat

2. **Cognition** – *'I'm going to have a panic attack'*
   'It will be awful'
   'I can't stand it'

3. **Imagery** – image of collapsing in public with a crowd of people looking at him

4. **Behaviour** – escape from the situation

TECHNIQUES AND INTERVENTIONS

Many techniques and interventions are used in multimodal therapy and training. Table 4.4 gives those most frequently used.

Table 4.4 *Frequently used techniques in multimodal therapy and training*

Modality	Therapy or training
Behaviour	Behaviour rehearsal
	Empty chair
	Exposure programme
	Fixed role therapy
	Modelling
	Paradoxical intention
	Psychodrama
	Reinforcement programmes
	Response prevention/cost
	Risk-taking exercises
	Self-monitoring and recording
	Stimulus control
	Shame-attacking
Affect	Anger expression/management
	Anxiety management
	Feeling-identification
Sensation	Biofeedback
	Hypnosis
	Meditation
	Relaxation training
	Sensate Focus Training
	Threshold training

Table 4.4 *continued*

Modality	Therapy or training
Imagery	Anti-future shock imagery
	Associated imagery
	Aversive imagery
	Coping imagery
	Implosion and imaginal exposure
	Positive imagery
	Rational emotive imagery
	Time projection imagery
Cognition	Bibliotherapy
	Challenging faulty inferences
	Cognitive rehearsal
	Coping statements
	Correcting misconceptions
	Disputing irrational beliefs
	Focusing
	Positive self-statements
	Problem-solving training
	Rational proselytizing
	Self-acceptance training
	Thought-stopping
Interpersonal	Assertion training
	Communication training
	Contracting
	Fixed role therapy
	Friendship/intimacy training
	Graded sexual approaches
	Paradoxical intentions
	Role play
	Social skills training
Drugs/Biology	Alcohol reduction programme
	Lifestyle changes, e.g. exercise, nutrition, etc.
	Referral to physicians or other specialists
	Stop smoking programme
	Weight reduction and maintenance programme

Sources: Palmer and Dryden, 1991; 1995; adapted from Lazarus, 1981

If applying a multimodal approach to stress management training, other techniques such as stress-mapping (Palmer, 1990), life and time management, stability zones and rituals (Palmer, 1989) can be included (see Table 4.5). A multimodal therapist would need a working knowledge of the different techniques. However, if the therapist is less experienced in some areas then a referral to another therapist or specialist may be required. Therefore a theoretical knowledge of the techniques available would be essential to make a 'judicious' referral when necessary. The Drugs/Biology modality may require training in exercise, nutrition and other health-related matters. Referral to medically trained practitioners is sometimes necessary. Multimodal therapists require good basic counselling skills in addition to their general working knowledge of techniques. Common sense helps too.

Table 4.5 *Stress management training*

Awareness of healthy stress (eustress) and unhealthy stress (distress) or pressure *v.* stress
Changing maladaptive cognitions and behaviour including Type A behaviour
Coping techniques
Emotional outlets
Formulation of a personal action plan
Life and time management
Occupational, organizational, family and social issues
Psychological, physiological and behavioural aspects of stress
Problem-solving techniques
Rational emotive behaviour therapy, ABCDE paradigm (*see Chapter 5*)
Recognition of stress in self and in others
Role play
Stability zones and rituals
Stress-mapping

Source: Adapted from Palmer, 1991

ADDITIONAL APPLICATIONS

Multimodal therapy and counselling has been applied to a range of clients in different settings which include helping alcohol abuse (Lazarus, 1965); schizophrenia (Lazarus, 1973b); career education (Gerler, 1977); children therapy (Keat, 1979); and marital/partner therapy (Lazarus, 1981). The author has also found the assessment procedure useful with clients diagnosed as suffering from post-traumatic stress disorder or athletes with performance anxiety. Multimodal group work is also undertaken. Group work is usually goal-orientated, task-orientated and time-limited (see Palmer and Dryden, 1995). Group members with help from the facilitator would formulate their own individual modality and structural profiles.

Palmer and Dryden (1995) have also applied a multimodal approach to stress management training in industry. A stress audit is usually instigated to ensure that the most appropriate intervention is undertaken (see Chapter 7). If a stress management or managing pressure course is a desired option then in a one- or two-day workshop the ABCDE paradigm of Ellis (see Chapter 5) can be taught; problems and symptoms can then be discussed; a structural profile produced for each delegate; and techniques and interventions covering the entire BASIC I.D. explored.

CONCLUSIONS

This chapter was intended to be a brief overview of multimodal therapy and counselling. It did not include multimodal techniques such as 'deserted island' or delve with any depth into bridging, second order BASIC I.D. assessment, or the different techniques suggested in Table 4.4. Similar to other broad-based eclectic psychotherapeutic approaches, multimodal therapy is multidimensional, multifactorial and multifaceted. The main difference is that in its assessment procedures specific attention is given to the entire seven modalities of the BASIC I.D. and nothing is left to chance or 'to the individual clinician's perspicacity' (Lazarus, 1988). The chapter is best concluded with a remark made by Lazarus (1990, p. 44):

> I have tried to provide a systematic, comprehensive psychotherapeutic structure that pragmatically contrives techniques, strategies and modalities, and addresses specific assessment and treatment operations. I have called this approach 'multimodal therapy' and offer it as a heuristic for diagnosing and treating discrete and interactive problems within and among each vector of personality.

REFERENCES

Bandura, A. (1986) *Social Foundations of Thoughts and Action: A Social Cognitive Theory*. Englewood Cliffs, NJ: Prentice-Hall.

Beitman, B.D. (1990) Why I am an integrationist (not an eclectic). In W. Dryden and J.C. Norcross (eds), *Eclecticism and Integration in Counselling and Psychotherapy*. Loughton: Gale Centre Publications.

Cox, T. (1978) *Stress*. London: Macmillan.

Cox, T. (1993) *Stress Research and Stress Management: Putting Theory to Work*. London: HMSO.

Cox, T. and Mackay, C.J. (1981) A transactional approach to occupational stress. In E.N. Corlett and J. Richardson (eds), *Stress, Work Design and Productivity*. Chichester: Wiley.

Dewe, P., Cox, T. and Ferguson, E. (1993) Individual strategies for coping with stress at work: A review of progress and directions for future research. *Work and Stress*, **7**, 5–15.

Gerler, E.R. (1977) The 'BASIC ID' in career education. *The Vocational Guidance Quarterly*, **25**, 238–44.

Grayson, J.B., Foa, E.B. and Steketee, G. (1985) Obsessive-compulsive disorder. In M. Hersen and A.S. Bellack (eds), *Handbook of Clinical Behavior Therapy with Adults*. New York: Plenum Press.

Karasu, T.B. (1986) The specificity versus nonspecificity dilemma: Toward identifying therapeutic change agents. *American Journal of Psychiatry*, **143**, 687–95.

Keat, D.B. (1979) *Multimodal Behavior Therapy with children.* New York: Pergamon Press.

Lazarus, A.A. (1965). Towards an Understanding and Effective Treatment of Alcoholism. *South African Medical Journal*, **39**, 736–41.

Lazarus, A.A. (1973a) 'Hypnosis' as a facilitator in behavior therapy. *International Journal of Clinical and Experimental Hypnosis*, **21**, 25–31.

Lazarus, A.A. (1973b) Multimodal behavior therapy: Treating the BASIC I.D. *Journal of Nervous and Mental Disease*, **156**, 404–11.

Lazarus, A.A. (1981) *The Practise of Multimodal Therapy.* New York: McGraw-Hill.

Lazarus, A.A. (1987) The Multimodal approach with adult outpatients. In N.S. Jacobson (ed.), *Psychotherapists in Clinical Practice.* New York: Guilford Press.

Lazarus, A.A. (1988) A multimodal perspective on the problem of sexual desire. In S.R. Leiblum and R.C. Rosen (eds), *Sexual Desire Problems.* New York: Guilford Press.

Lazarus, A.A. (1989) *The Practice of Multimodal Therapy.* Baltimore, MD: The Johns Hopkins University Press.

Lazarus, A.A. (1990) Why I am eclectic (not an integrationist). In W. Dryden and J.C. Norcross (eds), *Eclecticism and Integration in Counselling and Psychotherapy.* Loughton: Gale Centre Publications.

Lazarus, A.A. and Lazarus, C.N. (1991) *Multimodal Life History Inventory.* Champaign: Research Press.

Lazarus, R.S. (1966) *Psychological Stress and the Coping Process.* New York: McGraw-Hill.

Lazarus, R.S. and Folkman, S. (1984) *Stress, Appraisal and Coping.* New York: Springer.

London, P. (1964) *The Modes and Morals of Psychotherapy.* New York: Holt, Rinehart & Winston.

Marks, I. (1987) *Fears, Phobias and Rituals.* Oxford: Oxford University Press.

Norcross, J.C. and Grencavage, L.M. (1990) Eclecticism and integration in counseling and psychotherapy: Major themes and obstacles. In W. Dryden and J.C. Norcross (eds), *Eclecticism and Integration in Counselling and Psychotherapy.* Loughton: Gale Center Publications.

Palmer, S. (1989) The use of stability zones and rituals/routines to reduce or prevent stress. *Stress News*, **1**:3, 3–5.

Palmer, S. (1990) Stress mapping: A visual technique to aid counselling or training. *Employee Counselling Today*, **2**:2, 9–12.

Palmer, S. and Dryden, W. (1991) A multimodal approach to stress management. *Stress News*, 3:1, 2–10.

Palmer, S. (1991) Behaviour therapy and its application to stress management. *Health and Hygiene*, 12, 29–34.

Palmer, S. and Dryden, W (1995) *Counselling for Stress Problems.* London: Sage.

Smith, M.L., Glass, G.V. and Miller, T.I. (1980) *The Benefits of Psychotherapy.* Baltimore: The John Hopkins University Press.

CHAPTER 5

Rational Emotive Behaviour Therapy in the Treatment of Stress

Michael Abrams and Albert Ellis

Rational emotive behaviour therapists view stress-related disorders as originating in irrational beliefs (iB's), philosophies and attitudes, as opposed to the stressor. People who suffer from stress differ from people who suffer from emotional or neurotic problems mainly in that the stressed people have iB's about specific, short-term or more readily identifiable events, as opposed to the more mundane and diffuse difficulties suffered by the neurotic individual. Both the conscious and unconscious antecedents to stress difficulties and how they relate to distorted thinking and psychophysiological disorders are discussed from an information-processing perspective. Rational emotive behaviour treatments for stress-related disorders are detailed and explained.

INTRODUCTION

When mental health professionals examine stress as an object of treatment, we are really talking about the distress, both physical and emotional, that ensues from a series of interpersonal and environmental irritants, or a particularly compelling one. The term 'stress' is a broad or generic term applying to many different states and situations that act on the psyche and body to reduce homeostasis (Elliot and Einsdorfer, 1982). The lack of a consistent definition of stress makes any discussion of treatment difficult. After all, stress is not always bad. Yerkes and Dodson demonstrated this over a generation ago. Stress-related arousal frequently serves to enhance performance. In clinical work we typically use the term to apply to those pressures and strains of living that reduce the quality of life, and require changes in the individual to restore homeostasis. We shall also use the term to represent the result of several kinds of dysfunctional or irrational thinking.

DOES 'STRESS' EXIST?

The key issue for the rational emotive behaviour therapist is: how does the environmental irritation become oppressive? The answer is largely found within the stressed individual, not in the events. It is quite clear that the very same event will produce physiological or emotional arousal in one set of individuals and virtually no reaction in others. How then do the dysfunctional emotional and physical states that we call stress come about?

The answer is simple: stress does not exist. There is no iconoclasm intended here. We mean it quite literally: stress does not exist in itself. Stress is like good or evil: it exists only in its perceptions and reactions of the beholder (or the stressee). To quote Shakespeare:

> *Hamlet*: Why, then 'tis none to you; for there is nothing either good or bad but thinking makes it so ... (*Hamlet*, II. ii 259–61)

The evidence proves the same for stress. There is nothing intrinsically stressful or assuaging but thinking makes it so (Ellis and Abrahms, 1978). This is the foundation of the rational emotive behaviour treatment for stress-related and most emotional disorders (Ellis, 1962). Specifically, the rational emotive behaviour therapist works to bring the individual who is quite distressed by events in his or her environment to a state of mind similar to that of one who does not respond excessively to the same putative stressors. Only on rare occasions can a therapist help his or her client by eliminating their problem for them. The therapist is most effective in changing the client's reaction to the problem, which will tend to persist despite the best efforts of most clients and therapists. Specifically, the REBT therapist will seek first and pre-eminently to change the client's philosophies, attitudes and beliefs which lead to disturbance.

STRESS *V.* OTHER DISTURBANCES

Those who react to activating events (A's) with severe stress differ from those who have other disturbances in several key ways. First, stress tends to be more associated with physical illnesses or symptoms than do other psychological reactions. Second, stress reactions tend to be based on a single 'catastrophic' event or a group of noxious events that linger over time. This is in contrast to someone who suffers from, for example, chronic anxiety in which there tend to be a large array of activating events that ultimately lead to anxiety. In REBT terms, in stress reactions the A's are often more salient in the formula than the B's (the person's beliefs). This is particularly true of a particular kind of stress, post-traumatic stress disorder (PTSD), where the A's are so stark, unpredictable and harmful (such as rape, incest or torture) that a large percentage of 'normal' people, who would take less noxious events in good stride, tend to upset themselves severely and bring on terrifying flashbacks and nightmares for a period of years (Warren *et al.*, 1989; Warren *et al.*, 1990; Ellis, 1994).

Thus people with generalized anxiety require very little in the way of activating events (A's) to perpetuate their anxiety: their own compelling belief system about possible A's is usually sufficient. In contrast, the person suffering from a stress reaction can usually point to some objectively bad events that are the impetus of his or her malaise. This has the disadvantage of reinforcing the apparent connection between the A and the C. The stressed individual will conclude that '*my job is giving me an ulcer*', or '*my husband's temper is giving me these migraines*', and so on. As we will show later on, one prime goal of rational emotive behaviour therapy is to demonstrate to the client that the activating event does not by itself cause his or her psychological or psychophysiological consequence: his or her beliefs about the event do!

PHYSIOLOGICAL AND PSYCHOLOGICAL REACTIONS

Irrational beliefs and self-defeating styles are the essential origin of stress (Decker *et al.*, 1982; Vestre and Burnis, 1987; Forman *et al.*, 1987). However, the individual's particular reaction to stress tends to be constitutional. Let us examine for a moment the psychophysiological disorders that develop or worsen as a direct result of stress. These include digestive system ulcers, hypertension, migraine and tension headaches, lower back pain, temporo-mandibular joint syndrome, sciatica, lupus, multiple sclerosis, and others. We do not suggest that there is a linear correspondence between these stress-related illnesses and irrational beliefs. Rather, we have found that irrational beliefs are the foundation of the prolonged arousal and the emotional anguish that has been shown to be the prime cause of most ills associated with stress (Larbig, 1978; Woods and Lyons, 1990; Hart *et al.*, 1991).

The process by which irrational beliefs lead to psychophysiological disorders closely follows Selye's general adaption syndrome. The process begins with some activating event in the person's environment. The person then either consciously or unconsciously evaluates this event as good, bad, dangerous or unjust, based on his or her belief systems. At this point there follows arousal of the autonomic nervous system. With continued arousal, the weakest systems in the body begin to break down. The unconscious aspects of this process also make stress disorders more difficult to treat than those disorders in which there is a reaction to an overt problem.

REBT AND THE COGNITIVE PSYCHOLOGY OF STRESS

Since REBT is a cognitive-behavioural therapy, let us clarify what we mean by 'unconscious'. We do not refer to any dynamism (such as the id or the superego) taking direct action or direct control of behaviour. Instead we refer to several cognitive processes that are rapid and require minimal capacity. This principle was set forth by Donald Broadbent more than 35 years ago. He described the mind as a processing system with a limited capacity. That is, we can perceive only a small portion of what we sense, and we can consciously apprehend less than that. Just as we cannot be aware of all the external stimuli to which we are continually exposed, we cannot be simultaneously aware of all of our internal information.

The vast array of experiments utilizing priming methods and implicit learning methods demonstrate that we are not always at one with our mental database. Priming experiments reveal that our memorial stores can become activated without our awareness (Scarborough *et al.*, 1979; Jacoby and Dallas, 1981; Jacobs and Nadel,

1985). Implicit learning and memory experiments have shown that humans can acquire complex information without any knowledge of having done so (Abrams and Reber, 1988; Reber, 1989). Other cognitive processes that are not always accessible to consciousness are attitudes, biases, schemata and scripts that are quiescent and unconscious until activated. At that time they influence consciousness rapidly and indirectly, but they are not independent of will. With effort they can be ascertained and, if appropriate, disputed, and replaced with new attitudes, scripts and schemata.

Kahneman *et al.* (1982) demonstrated that most of us form judgements based on what may be faulty heuristics. They further warned that our acquisition of these heuristics may be involuntary. They and their co-workers have failed to show, however, that if a person is made aware that he or she is making judgements based on a faulty heuristic, and is given an alternative means of making a judgement, he or she will not do so. In most cases, he or she will.

We all possess these underlying prejudices but are only aware of them if they are addressed in some fashion. Most people do not think about how they feel about thin people or fat people until they come upon one of them. Their unconscious attitudes are not inaccessible but can act directly on behaviour without directly entering verbal awareness. Other unconscious cognitive processes involve more specific judgements about individuals. We frequently make assessments about a person's nature, beauty or honesty after only a brief view of his or her face. These assessments, too, tend to be based on unconscious judgements (Lewicki, 1985; 1986). Another important phenomenon is based on the declarative-procedural-knowledge distinction. This model shows that we have the ability and knowledge necessary to perform many tasks without any conscious awareness of having it (Cohen and Squire, 1980; Cohen and Corkin, 1981; Jacoby and Witherspoon, 1982). In fact, there is research which indicates that many experts really do not know how they are able to do what they do so well (Nisbett and Wilson, 1977).

In general, then, what we call unconscious, the experimental psychologists tend to refer to as those stages of information processing that occur outside of awareness. In almost all cases these unconscious processes can be made conscious with effort. A similar process occurs in somatoform disorders which tend to occur with high frequency among stress sufferers (Lipowski, 1988; Frost *et al.*, 1988). In these cases the stressed individual begins to exhibit physical symptoms that cannot be clearly pinned down. Of course, many people actually become ill, but are not accurately diagnosed. But those who feel ill without actually being so, do so because of their own beliefs. One of our clients exemplifies this:

THE CASE OF GAETANO

Gaetano was referred to the clinic of the Institute for Rational-Emotive Therapy in New York. He had been suffering from severe pains in his neck and jaw. He had consulted an otolaryngologist and a neurologist as well as his family physician. Exhaustive medical testing failed to discover any organic basis for his symptoms.

During therapy Gaetano revealed that he had come from Italy as an adolescent, and was raised in the USA with conservative Italian values. He eventually did quite well as a construction manager, and married an American-born businesswoman.

Over time the conflict between their two cultures began to greatly distress Gaetano. His wife, Gloria, was 'too domineering and too independent'. She came and went as she pleased, and never accepted his authority as 'the man' of the household. This led him to create an increasingly violent rage that he had great trouble acknowledging. After a few sessions, he said he had fantasies of killing her. When asked why he did not simply divorce her, he said he could not do so.

The house they lived in was where Gaetano had been raised, and the house his father had died in. To give it up would be both painful and humiliating. He said he could not stand the idea that Gloria could end up owning it: this would be a terrible indignity he could not bear. Thus Gaetano had locked himself into what Miller (1944) called an avoidance-avoidance conflict. He strongly 'needed' to avoid his wife, but he also 'needed' to avoid the hassles inherent in ending his hated marriage. He began picking up women in bars and sleeping with them in motels. By doing this he felt he was getting justice for the pain his wife was putting him through, but in turn he suffered great guilt. So, feeling trapped, he began to express himself through his neck and jaw pains.

The process by which his situation was converted to physical symptoms began with his irrational beliefs. Some of these were:

(1) 'I *cannot stand* to be with Gloria one more moment.'
(2) 'I *must* get rid of her, even if I have to kill her.'
(3) 'Wanting to kill my wife makes me a *terrible person*.'
(4) 'I *must* not lose my house, it would make me *a fool*.'
(5) 'It would be *terrible* and dangerous if I let my rage show.'
(6) 'I *must* punish her by sleeping with other women.'
(7) 'I'm a *terrible worthless man* for cheating on my wife.'

The irrational beliefs about Gaetano's marriage were like a series of cul-de-sacs. He was trapped, and his growing rage led to increased anxiety and physical tension. But two other factors led to the symptomology, the first being constitutional. Some people appear to possess the innate tendency to express emotions through physical symptoms (Templer and Lester, 1974; Suls and Rittenhouse, 1987). This notion is not new. Alexander (1950) proposed that people with these disorders have a biological predisposition to bring them on. Gaetano probably had this tendency: otherwise he would have probably expressed his distress in more traditional ways.

The second factor was Gaetano's beliefs and feelings about inescapable catastrophe. He saw this as too terrible to be real, so he literally denied its existence, and instead focused on a part of his body that was reacting in a typical way to his stress. The muscle tension in his jaw and head that commonly accompanies many stress reactions was interpreted as an illness. The focus on his illness distracted him from, even relieved him of, the pain of his apparently inescapable dilemma.

Thus when people perceive stressors as being so terrible as to fall outside the domain of any conceivable life event, they may tend to dissociate. In REBT terms, psychophysiological and somatoform disorders often result from extreme awfulizing, combined with some additional irrational beliefs. These beliefs may be to the effect that 'something bad absolutely will happen to me!' or 'any physical symptom proves something terrible is happening to my body!'

Gaetano's therapy focused on three aspects of his difficulty. The first was the system of beliefs that he was in a terrible situation. He was helped to see that although his situation was bad, it was far from so bad as to make life unbearable. He was shown how to increase his frustration tolerance so that he could 'stand' to be with his wife until a way out of his circumstances could be found.

His second set of irrational beliefs, that *he absolutely must not* be enraged and have fantasies of revenge, led to his self-downing. He was shown that although it would have been preferable for him to accept his wife's disagreeable ways without rage, he was not a bad person for feeling enraged. He was also shown that his wife was not the absolutely bad person he was making her out to be, simply because she differed from him and because he could no longer tolerate her.

The final aspect of Gaetano's therapy helped him to work on practical solutions. He was encouraged to tell his wife how he felt and to consult an attorney. After a couple of painful months of legal and domestic negotiations, she agreed to a divorce, and he was able to keep the house. His symptoms vanished.

IRRATIONAL BELIEFS AND STRESS

Rational emotive behaviour therapy (REBT) predicates its treatment of most neurotic problems on the hypothesis that humans, to varying degrees, endorse and act on convictions that are self- and socially-defeating. These partially learned and partly constructed irrational beliefs lead to a significant portion of psychological difficulties. There are other factors involved in mental disorders, but these can only be partially addressed with psychotherapy. The other causes are genetic, biochemical and structural. Psychotherapy indirectly treats these other ailments in the same way that it helps with other problems of life that are unyielding – by helping people change what they can change, and accept and endure what they cannot change.

REBT uses a simple model in its system of therapy: the ABCDE model. The A refers to an unfortunate activating event in people's lives that results in a dysfunctional behavioural or emotional reaction. B is the belief system that largely determines or regulates their response to the A. C is their disturbed consequence to the A and B. D refers to the disputing that challenges their irrational disturbance-creating beliefs. Finally, E is their effective new philosophy that they are encouraged to adopt.

In most discussions of REBT, the C (consequences) refers to emotional reactions. However, in the case of stress the C is often organic or physical symptoms. This is very similar to the model of stress adopted by the National Academy of Sciences (Dollahite, 1991) which expressed stress reactions in terms of an xyz model. In their version they refer to the x as the *potential activator*, the y as the individual's *reactions* to the potential activator, and the z as the *consequence* of the x's and y's. The authors also label interactions between the x's and y's as *mediators*. These researchers came to the same conclusion that I (Albert Ellis) came to in 1955. External events do not by themselves result in disturbance – whether stress or any other kind. The range of reactions to unpropitious events is so wide that people's perceptions and evaluations of these events are the prime mediators of their reaction (Ellis, 1962; 1978; 1985a; 1988; 1991; Ellis and Dryden, 1987).

The cognitive process that facilitates the creation of stress almost always involves irrational beliefs (Woods, 1987; Vestre and Burnis, 1987; Forman, 1990; Henry *et al.*, 1991). These have been detailed extensively in previous articles and books, but briefly they include rigid, inflexible and usually unexamined beliefs, personal philosophies and attitudes that we all possess to varying degrees. These can take the form of unconditional demands, such as: 'I *have* to be successful!'; 'All people who have hurt me *must* be severely punished!'; 'I *absolutely must* be physically competent and healthy or life is terrible!'

Negatively distorted judgements (awfulizing) are also efficient stress producers. Some typical ones are: 'It would be *awful* if I were to lose this case!'; 'I *couldn't stand* to be fired'; 'I am *totally worthless* if I lose my business!'

Beliefs based on absolute social needs commonly produce stress reactions. People create traps for themselves with musts that often cannot be satisfied: 'I *must* get the respect of or love from all significant people!'; 'Other people *must* respect my needs!'

Stress reactions to irrational thinking differ in one important way from other disturbed consequences (C) in that the stressed individual tends to link a number of irrational conclusions together into an overwhelming whole. The woman who is vying for a promotion and is asked to produce a key business report on a near-impossible deadline, all the while seeking to get home early enough to get her child out of day care, will tend to experience stress. But let us examine the underlying beliefs and demands that transform these social pressures into her experience of stress. The stress process begins with her compelling desire to get the promotion, which becomes the demand: 'I *must* get a promotion and I will be a *total failure* if I blow it!' or 'I *must* get the promotion or I'll never get anywhere!' Next, she becomes aware of the deadline, and further elevates her arousal with a belief like: 'If I don't get the report in by tonight, they'll know I'm not competent, and that would be *awful*!' or 'I'll never get it done right in the time they have given me, and they'll see what an *incompetent person* I am!'

Research has provided compelling evidence that complex cognitive processes, like speech, becomes automatic and extremely rapid with repetition (Posner and Snyder, 1974). Thus habitual statements, like the preceding, will at times be subtle and rapid. So it requires effort to first bring them into awareness and then to practise disputing them once we clearly see them. Without the effort to understand these irrational cognitions, we are at their mercy. As noted above, experimental psychology has demonstrated that many judgements occur rapidly, and sometimes outside of awareness, and that they often result in emotional changes (Foster and Grovier, 1978; Kunst-Wilson and Zajonc, 1980; Zajonc, 1984). It is difficult, if not impossible, to physically control these reactions. But a change in personal philosophy ultimately leads to the cognitive changes that can bring them under control.

TREATMENT

Rational emotive behaviour therapy uses a large number of cognitive, emotive and behavioural techniques to help people who over-react to stressors and who add to their appropriate feelings of concern, displeasure and frustration about these stressors, inappropriate, self-defeating feelings of severe stress, anxiety and panic. Thus, rational emotive behaviour practitioners often use biofeedback and relaxation techniques (Fried and Golden, 1989; Fried, 1990), hypnosis (Ellis, 1985b; Stanton, 1989), self-instructional training (Meichenbaum, 1977), meditation and yoga (Benson, 1975; Ellis, 1984; Goleman, 1993), behavioural exercises (Ellis and Abrahms, 1978) and other methods that other therapists use.

In addition to these traditional methods, REBT usually includes a number of special cognitive techniques, especially active-directive disputing (D) of clients' dysfunctional and irrational beliefs (B). Thus, when a rational emotive behaviour therapist works with someone suffering from stress-related disorders, the first step usually involves finding the events that the client is making stressful. The next critical step involves finding the beliefs, attitudes and personal philosophies by which clients convert the perceptions to dysphoria. It is this aspect of REBT that most tests the skill of the therapist.

Many clients seeking help for stress-related disorders feel trapped by the events that are distressing them. They typically have strong convictions in the absolute badness of these happenings. Therapists therefore need to be sensitive and cautious in challenging these beliefs. Clients suffering from severe stressors are convinced, either overtly or implicitly, that these 'terrible' things are the direct and only cause of their problems. Helping them come to see that the things are indeed bad but that their 'terribleness' is largely their own creation will be resisted unless therapists first establish that they empathetically accept the clients' suffering as real. Perhaps the worst thing any therapist can do is to dismiss a particular stressor as 'insignificant' or 'minor'. If the client perceives it as monumental, the therapist had better accept this as the starting point.

The next step is to find the specific beliefs, philosophies and attitudes that create stress. This can be accomplished by interviewing clients about their feelings when they encounter stressors. Once their disturbed emotions are clarified, the therapist in collaboration with the client probes for the irrational beliefs and dogmas that create stress reactions, and shows clients how to actively and forcefully dispute (D) these beliefs (B).

More specifically, REBT teaches clients how to do the following disputing:

- *Disputing absolute musts*: 'Why *must* I always succeed and experience no unfortunate hassles'? *Answer*: 'I never *have* to succeed, though I would very much *prefer* to do so. I really *have to* experience many unfortunate hassles because that is the nature of normal living. It's too damned bad – but hardly *awful* or *terrible*.'
- *Disputing I-can't-stand-it-itis*: 'Where is the evidence that I *can't stand* these stressors that are now occurring?' *Answer*: 'Only in my nutty head! I won't die of them and can be happy in spite of them. They're not *horrible* but only bearably painful!'
- *Disputing feeling of worthlessness*: 'Is it true that I am an inadequate, *worthless* person if I do not handle stressful conditions well and even make them worse?' *Answer*: 'No, I am a person who may well be acting inadequately at this time in this respect but I am never a totally *worthless* (or good) person, just a fallible human who is doing my best to cope with difficult conditions.'

As REBT shows people how to look for their absolutist shoulds, oughts and musts, and for their awfulizing, can't-stand-it-itis and self-downing about the stressors that they experience, it also employs a number of other cognitive methods that it has invented or adopted to help people change their dysfunctional thinking for more effective and less disturbing thinking. Thus it uses reframing, and shows clients how to find good things in some of the bad things that happen to them and how to accept the challenge of not upsetting themselves when they are under unusual stress. It helps them, when they procrastinate or are addicted to harmful feelings and behaviours, to referent a number of disadvantages of what they are doing and to forcefully go over them several times a day, so as to plant them into their consciousness. It 'works out' with clients' coping rational self-statements, particularly philosophical ones, that they keep using to face some of the worst stressors and to refuse to upset themselves. Such as: 'Yes, I am really under great strain right now and there is nothing that I can do about relieving some of it, but I don't have to eliminate it and I *can* lead a reasonable happy life even if these difficulties continue.'

Rational emotive behaviour therapy encourages clients to do cognitive homework, including the steady filling out of the REBT Self-Help Form (Sichel and Ellis, 1984). This helps them to find and dispute their irrational beliefs. It provides them with psychoeducational materials, such as pamphlets, books and audiovisual cassettes, that show them how to use rational emotive anti-disturbing and problem-solving methods (Ellis, 1975; 1978; 1988; Ellis and Harper, 1975). It encourages them to record their therapy sessions and to listen to these several times. It pushes them to learn REBT methods and to teach them to others, so as to implant them into their own hearts and heads. It shows them how to model themselves after other individuals who have coped well with stressors.

Rational emotive behaviour therapy always uses a number of emotive-evocative, dramatic methods to help individuals cope with stress situations. Thus it teaches them how to use rational emotive imagery (Maultsby, 1971), in the course of which they work on their disturbed feelings when they imagine a very stressful event happening, and change these to appropriate feelings of sorrow, regret and frustration. It encourages them to do its famous shame-attacking exercises (Ellis, 1973; 1988) and learn to deliberately do foolish and ridiculous acts in public and not to upset themselves or put themselves down when others disapprove of them for doing these acts. It shows them how to create and use very forceful and dramatic coping statements to change some of their disturbance-creating thoughts and feelings. It encourages them to tape record some of their worst irrational beliefs and to strongly dispute them on tape, and then let their therapists and other people listen to their disputations to see how forceful they really are. It provides them with rational humorous songs and other humorous ways of interfering with their taking stressors too seriously (Ellis, 1987).

Behaviourally, REBT employs a number of action methods to help people overcome their overly stressful reactions to the difficulties of their lives. Thus, it encourages them to use *in vivo* desensitization and exposure methods to overcome some of their irrational fears. It shows them how they can deliberately stay in poor situations (e.g. remain in a job where their supervisor is hostile and negative) until they give up their own feelings of horror and terror – and then decide whether to leave these situations. It shows them how they can reinforce themselves when they do REBT homework that they agree to do and penalize themselves when they fail to do it. It gives them skill training in important areas where they feel very stressed, so that they will function better and enjoy themselves more in these areas. Thus it often provides clients with assertion, communication, relationship and social skills training.

As usual, then, rational emotive behaviour therapy uses a good number of cognitive, emotive and behavioural methods, some of which are special to REBT, to help people make their lives less stressful and to cope with stressors that they cannot change. It especially tries to help them push themselves to improve unpleasant social and environmental situations; but to unconditionally accept themselves, other people and the world, even when unusually stressful conditions persist. As Hauck (1977) points out, when people are faced with unpleasant situations, they have three main choices: to change, to stay with or to leave them. Whichever of these choices they make, REBT endeavors to help them accomplish it with a minimum of stress or emotional disturbance. Severe stressors are often inevitable; undue stress about them is not.

REFERENCES

Abrams, M. and Reber, A.S. (1988) Implicit learning: robustness in the face of psychiatric disorders. *Journal of Psycholinguistic Research*, **17**, 425–39.

Alexander, F. (1950) *Psychosomatic Medicine: Its Principles and Applications*. New York: Norton.

Benson, H. (1975) *The Relaxation Response*. New York: Morrow.

Cohen, J.J. and Corkin, S. (1981) The amnesic patient, H.M.: Learning and retention of a cognitive skill. *Society for Neuroscience Abstracts*, **7**, 235.

Cohen, K.M. and Squire, L.R. (1980) Preserved learning and retention of pattern-analyzing skill in amnesia: Dissociation of knowing how and knowing that. *Science*, **210**, 207–10.

Decker, T.W., Williams, J.M. and Hall, D. (1982) Preventive training in management of stress for reduction of physiological symptoms through increased cognitive and behavioral controls. *Psychological Reports*, **50**, 1327–34.

Dollahite, D.C. (1991) Family resource management and family stress theories: Toward a conceptual integration. *Lifestyles*, **12**, 361–77.

Elliot, G.R. and Einsdorfer, C. (1982) *Stress and Human Health: Analysis and Implications of Research*. New York: Springer.

Ellis, A. (1962) *Reason and Emotion in Psychotherapy*. Secaucus, NJ: Citadel.

Ellis, A. (1975) *How to Live With a Neurotic: at Home and at Work* (Hollywood, CA, Wilshire Books).

Ellis, A. (1973) How to stubbornly refuse to be ashamed of anything (cassette recording). Institute for Rational-Emotive Therapy, New York.

Ellis, A. (1978) What people can do for themselves to cope with stress. In C.L. Cooper and R. Payne (eds), *Stress at Work*, pp. 209–22. New York: Wiley.

Ellis, A. (1984) The place of meditation in cognitive-behavior therapy and rational-emotive therapy. In D.H. Shapiro and R. Walsh (eds), *Meditation*, pp. 671–3. New York: Aldine.

Ellis, A. (1985a) *Overcoming Resistance: Rational-Emotive Therapy with Difficult Clients*. New York: Springer.

Ellis, A. (1985b) Anxiety about anxiety: the use of hypnosis with rational-emotive therapy. In E.T. Dowd and J.M. Healy (eds), *Case Studies in Hypnotherapy*, pp. 1–11. New York: Guilford Press.

Ellis, A. (1987) The use of rational humorous songs in psychotherapy. In W.F. Fry, Jr and W.A. Salameh (eds), *Handbook of Humor and Psychotherapy*, pp. 265–86. Sarasota, FL: Professional Resource Exchange.

Ellis, A. (1988) *How to Stubbornly Refuse to Make Yourself Miserable About Anything – Yes, Anything*. Secaucus, NJ: Lyle Stuart.

Ellis, A. (1991) The revised ABC's of rational-emotive therapy (RET). *Journal of Rational-Emotive and Cognitive Behavior Therapy*, **9**, 139–72.

Ellis, A. (1994) Post-traumatic stress disorder: A rational emotive behavioral theory. *Journal of Rational-Emotive and Cognitive Behavior Therapy*, **72**, 3–25.

Ellis, A. and Abrahms, E. (1978) *Brief Psychotherapy in Medical and Health Practice*. New York: Springer.

Ellis, A. and Dryden, W. (1987) *The Practice of Rational-Emotive Therapy*. New York: Springer.

Ellis, A. and Harper, R.A. (1975) *A New Guide to Rational Living*. North Hollywood, C A: Wilshire Books.

Forman, S.G. (1990) Rational-emotive therapy: Contributions to teacher stress management. *School Psychology Review*, **19**, 315–21.

Forman, M.A., Tosi, D.J. and Rudy, D.R. (1987) Common irrational beliefs associated with the psychophysiological conditions of low back pain, peptic ulcers and migraine headache: A multivariate study. *Journal of Rational-Emotive Therapy*, **5**, 255–65.

Foster, J.A. and Grovier, E. (1978) Discrimination without awareness? *Quarterly Journal of Experimental Psychology*, **30**, 282–95.

Fried, R. (1990) Integrating music in breathing training and relaxation: ii. Applications. *Biofeedback and Self Regulation*, **15**, 171–7.

Fried, R. and Golden, W.L. (1989) The role of psychophysiological hyperventilation assessment in cognitive behavior therapy. *Journal of Cognitive Psychotherapy: an International Quarterly*, **3**, 5–14.

Frost, R.O., Morgenthau, J.E., Riessman, C.K. and Whalen, M. (1988) Somatic response to stress, physical symptoms and health service use: The role of current stress. *Behaviour Research and Therapy*, **26**, 481–7.

Goleman, D. (1993) A slow medical calming of the mind. *The New York Times Magazine*, March 21.

Hart, K.E., Turner, S.H., Hittner, J.B. and Cardozo, S.R. (1991) Life stress and anger: Moderating effects of type A irrational beliefs. *Personality and Individual Differences*, **12**, 557–60.

Hauck, P.A. (1977) *Marriage is a Loving Business*. Philadelphia: Westminster.

Henry, B.M., Gonzalez de Rivera, J.L., de las Cuevas, C. and Gonzalez, I. (1991) El indice de reactividad al estres en pacientes asmaticos cronicos (The stress reactivity index in chronic asthmatic patients). *Psiquis: Revista de Psiquiatria, Psicologia y Psicosomatica*, **12**, 20–5.

Jacobs, W.J. and Nadel, L. (1985) Stress induced recovery of fears and phobias. *Psychological Review*, **92**, 512–31.

Jacoby, L.L. and Dallas, M. (1981) On the relationship between autobiographical memory and perceptual learning. *Journal of Experimental Psychology: General*, **110**, 306–40.

Jacoby, L.L. and Witherspoon, D. (1982) Remembering without awareness. *Canadian Journal of Psychology*, **32**, 300–24.

Kahneman, D., Slovic, P. and Tversky, A. (1982) *Judgement Under Uncertainty: Heuristics and Biases*. New York: Cambridge University Press.

Kunst-Wilson, W.R. and Zajonc, R.B. (1980) Affective discrimination of stimuli that cannot be recognized. *Science*, **207**, 557–8.

Larbig, W. (1978) Psychophysiological approach to etiology and the therapy of psychosomatic disorders. *Zeitschrift fur Psychosomatische Medizin und Psychoanalyse*, **24**, 355–67.

Lewicki, P. (1985) Nonconscious biasing effects of single instances on subsequent judgements. *Journal of Personality and Social Psychology*, **48**, 563–74.

Lewicki, P. (1986) *Nonconscious Social Information Processing*. Orlando, FL: Academic Press.

Lipowski, Z.J. (1988) Somatization: The concept and its clinical application. *American Journal of Psychiatry*, **145**, 1358–68.

Maultsby, M.C., Jr (1971) Rational emotive imagery. *Rational Living*, **6**, 24–7.

Meichenbaum, D. (1977) *Cognitive-Behavior Modification*. New York: Plenum Press.

Miller, N.E. (1944) Experimental studies of conflict. In J. McV. Hunt (ed.), *Personality and Behavior Disorders*. New York: Ronald Press.

Nisbett, R.E. and Wilson, T.D. (1977) Telling more than we can know: Verbal reports on mental processes. *Psychological Review*, **84**, 231–59.

Posner, M.I. and Snyder, C.R.R. (1974) Attention and cognitive control. In P.M.A. Rabbit and S. Dornic (eds), *Information Processing and Cognition: The Loyola Symposium*. Hillsdale, NJ: Erlbaum.

Reber, A.S. (1989) Implicit learning and tacit knowledge. *Journal of Experimental Psychology: General*, **118**, 219–35.

Scarborough, D.L., Gerard, L. and Cortese, C. (1979) Accessing lexical memory: The transfer of word repetition effects across task and modality. *Memory and Cognition*, **7**, 3–12.

Sichel, J. and Ellis, A. (1984) *RET Self-Help Form*. New York: Institute for Rational-Emotive Therapy.

Stanton, H.E. (1989) Stressreduktion durch rational-emotive therapie und hypnoseinduktion (Stress relief through rational-emotive therapy and hypnotic induction). *Experimentelle und Klinische Hypnose*, **5**, 83–90.

Suls, J. and Rittenhouse, J.D. (1987) Personality and physical health: An introduction (In special issue: Personality and physical health). *Journal of Personality*, **55**, 155–67.

Templer, D.I. and Lester, D. (1974) Conversion disorders: A review of research findings. *Comprehensive Psychiatry*, **15**, 285–94.

Vestre, N.D. and Burnis, J.J. (1987) Irrational beliefs and the impact of stressful life events. *Journal of Rational-Emotive Therapy*, **5**, 183–8.

Warren, R., Zgourides, G. and Jones, A. (1989) Cognitive bias and irrational belief as predictors of avoidance. *Behaviour Research and Therapy*, **27**, 181–8.

Warren, R., Zgourides, G. and Englert, M. (1990) Relationships between catastrophic cognitions and body sensations in anxiety disordered, mixed diagnosis, and normal subjects. *Behaviour Research and Therapy*, **28**, 355–7.

Woods, P.J. (1987) Reductions in type A behavior, anxiety, anger, and physical illness as related to changes in irrational beliefs: results of a demonstration project in industry. *Journal of Rational-Emotive Therapy*, **5**, 213–37.

Woods, P.J. and Lyons, L.C. (1990) Irrational beliefs and psychosomatic disorders (In special issue: Cognitive-behavior therapy with physically ill people: i). *Journal of Rational-Emotive & Cognitive Behavior Therapy*, **8**, 3–20.

Zajonc, R.B. (1984) On the primacy of affect. *American Psychologist*, **39**, 117–23.

CHAPTER 6

Traumatic Stress at Work: A Public Health Model

David Richards

The emergence of the 'new public health' movement provides a framework for an integrated and co-ordinated policy for responding to traumatic stress in the workplace. A review of the clinical literature on post-traumatic stress reveals that the components of this framework are available: the challenge is to put in place all the various elements. An organizational response is described which tries to use primary, secondary and tertiary prevention strategies to reduce the impact of traumatic incidents – in this case, armed robberies – on employees of a financial services company. Interdepartmental working, appropriate use of management and social support, pre-trauma training and cognitive-behavioural counselling techniques are all used in an attempt to tailor support to the individual's own needs. Binding the process together is a simple psychological health screening process, offering as a by-product information to improve the responsiveness of the service.

INTRODUCTION

Many working environments contain the potential for violent or traumatic incidents. This threat is particularly acute for anyone handling money as a day-to-day part of their work. With more than 30 armed robberies happening every week in Britain, the threat of robbery is a daily fact of life for staff working in banks and building societies.

The impact of traumatic events such as rape, physical assault, combat, fire and other disasters has been known for centuries. Shakespeare has Lady Percy asking forlornly of her husband Harry Hotspur's disturbed sleep, the 'beads of sweat' upon his brow and the way he 'starts so often when he sit'st alone' (Alexander, 1978, pp. 489–90). Hotspur was a man tormented by his combat experiences. There are many other allusions to post-traumatic stress in historical sources, including Samuel Pepys's difficulty with sleeplessness and nightmares after the great fire of London (Cohen, 1991).

Despite this wealth of folk knowledge, it was not until 1980 that a universal description of post-traumatic stress occurred in the psychiatric diagnostic handbooks (American Psychiatric Association, 1994). The concept of post-traumatic stress disorder (PTSD) as a homogeneous syndrome reliably arising after many different types of trauma came from work in the USA, mainly with Vietnam veterans and rape survivors. There may be argument still as to the details of the symptomatology, but it is now almost universally accepted that PTSD is a specific disorder and distinct from other conditions such as depression, phobias or panic.

Three distinct groups of symptoms are known to arise after a traumatic event – intrusive, avoidant and arousal symptoms. These are summarized in Table 6.1. Furthermore, the definition of PTSD maintains that one must have experienced 'intense fear, helplessness and horror' before the diagnosis can be arrived at, reflecting the emphasis on extreme stress in the diagnosis of PTSD.

Table 6.1 *DSM-IV symptoms of post-traumatic stress disorder*

Re-experiencing symptoms
   1. Recurrent, intrusive, distressing recollections
   2. Repetitive nightmares
   3. Flashbacks
   4. Reactive psychological distress
   5. Reactive psychological arousal

Circumscribed avoidance and dissociative mechanisms
   1. Avoidance of thoughts and feelings
   2. Avoidance of activities and situations
   3. Psychogenic amnesia
   4. Diminished interest
   5. Detachment from others
   6. Restricted range of affect
   7. Sense of foreshortened future

Heightened arousal
   1. Sleep disturbance
   2. Irritability and anger
   3. Concentration difficulties
   4. Hypervigilance
   5. Exaggerated startle response

PREVALENCE AND NATURAL HISTORY OF POST-TRAUMATIC STRESS

Many studies have attempted to estimate how many people suffer from the after-effects of traumatic incidents. There are only a few general population studies looking at community prevalence, putting the rate at between 1% and 1.3% of the population (Helzer *et al.*, 1987; Davidson *et al.*, 1991). Disasters, however, have provided researchers with a rich source of data, giving estimates of between 22% and 50% (e.g. Raphael, 1986; Curran *et al.*, 1990).

The general population prevalence figures represent a rate that is equivalent to the diagnostic prevalence of schizophrenia in the USA. The other studies show great variance in prevalence estimates, which are due to population and methodological differences. After reviewing the evidence, the Disasters Working Party estimated that after a disaster: '40–70% experience distress in the first month; 24–40% experience distress after the first year; 15–20% experience chronic levels of anxiety which remain high for longer than 2 years' (Home Office, 1991). Within the banks and building societies, our own work (Richards and Deale, 1990) and that of others (N. Murray, personal communication) has suggested that a long-term prevalence rate of 25% may exist in the industry for people who have experienced robberies, a rate which accords with the studies outlined above.

The effect of time on post-traumatic stress symptoms is illustrated by a study of rape survivors in Philadelphia (Rothbaum et al., 1992). Although one cannot have a formal diagnosis of PTSD until a month has elapsed post-trauma, symptomatic criteria for PTSD were met by 94% of 64 women survivors of rape interviewed within 12 days of the assault. In subsequent interviews over the next three to four months, the incidence rate had dropped to 47% by the final interview. Furthermore, those women who had the most severe initial symptoms were more likely to have a diagnosis of persistent PTSD at the three-to-four-month point. Most of the recovery seemed to take place during the first four weeks, and for the most severe group little evidence of recovery was seen after this time. The authors state that 'rape victims who do not evidence substantial recovery within one month post-rape are likely to continue to suffer from PTSD' (p. 471).

The importance of these data for an integrated approach to post-traumatic stress is that if high levels of chronic symptoms are present one to two months post-trauma, they are unlikely to remit spontaneously. However, such individuals can be identified within the first month post-trauma and targeted for intervention.

THE NEW PUBLIC HEALTH

We are currently seeing the emergence of a vigorous public health movement, the so-called 'new public health'. Both the King's Fund (Jacobson et al., 1991) and the Government (Department of Health, 1991) have published papers with clearly specified targets for health promotion and preventive health. The old 'is it lifestyle or is it environment?' debate has given way to a new understanding of the complexity of key health determinants. The 'new public health' integrates primary prevention (lifestyle and environmental changes to prevent disease), secondary prevention (detection of early signs of disease and action to contain problems at this stage) and tertiary prevention (action to treat existing disorder and limit handicap where disorders are chronic) (Ashton and Seymour, 1988).

The 'new public health' movement, therefore, does not distinguish between prevention and cure. It is within its remit to address health at all stages of disease progression as well as taking action to prevent problems in the first place.

Can the 'new public health' movement provide a framework for managing traumatic stress in the workplace? An examination of the counselling and therapy literature on traumatic stress does indeed indicate that all the elements of a public health package exist. The challenge, therefore, is to integrate the different elements in a comprehensive way.

PTSD: COUNSELLING AND TREATMENT

The literature describing counselling and treatment for PTSD is characterized by a profusion of case-studies and descriptions of therapy but a paucity of carefully evaluated treatment studies. Controlled studies are rarer still.

Counselling

Counselling has become a widespread response to traumatic incidents, particularly for those people suffering from acute reactions to trauma. It is now commonplace to have psychological 'debriefing' (Dyregrov, 1989) for survivors immediately post-disaster, although this is not usually available for others involved in less public traumas such as traffic accidents. Debriefing, often in groups, involves the counsellor facilitating the survivor's ability to recount their experiences factually and emotionally. Despite the widespread use of this method, there is little evidence as to its effect, resulting in Lane (1991) calling for 'mutually-supportive professional practice, underpinned by systematic evaluative research' (p. 21). When a debriefing-style psychotherapy was used with long-term PTSD, only 30% average improvement rates were found (Thompson, 1993). From this work, Thompson at the Middlesex Hospital's Stress Clinic regards 30% improvement as the benchmark to which one compares any other form of therapy. Similarly, Israeli army experience showed that 40% of battle-shock casualties still went on to develop chronic PTSD despite intensive debriefing (Noy *et al.*, 1984; Solomon, 1989).

Another type of counselling approach frequently used is grief or bereavement counselling. This is the approach favoured by Hodgkinson and Stewart (1991), two workers heavily involved with survivors and those bereaved after the *Herald of Free Enterprise* disaster. Here, the sufferer is helped to integrate (or 'accept') their loss into their lives. Although this is useful with bereavement, it appears less so for PTSD, and little data are available to evaluate this approach with survivors of trauma.

Most counsellors now recognize the difference between acute reactions to severe stress and the long-term chronic nature of PTSD. Duckworth was involved in one of the earliest public disasters – the Bradford City Football Club fire – which alerted people to the large number of psychological casualties. He has noted that 'post-traumatic problems require counselling/treatment which go far beyond the ordinary "non-directive" counselling approach' (Duckworth and Charlesworth, 1988, p. 207).

Pharmacological treatment

Changes have been detected in biological markers such as noradrenaline and endogenous opiates in people with PTSD. Several authors (Kolb, 1987; Van der Kolk, 1987; Friedman, 1988) have postulated psychobiological mechanisms for

PTSD and have made subsequent predictions about pharmacological treatment.

Treatments have concentrated on sedative drugs such as diazepam (valium) (Van der Kolk *et al.*, 1985) and anti-depressants. The literature includes controlled studies by Frank *et al.*, 1988b and Reist *et al.*, 1989. The first, comparing two anti-depressants with a placebo, claimed that specific PTSD symptoms were improved. The other showed that improvement was probably due to general mood improvement, not to the effect of the drugs on PTSD symptoms *per se*. In both studies many PTSD symptoms remained after treatment, and the studies did not include an evaluation of symptoms when the drugs had been stopped.

The main disadvantages of sedative drugs are the dangers of dependence and subsequent withdrawal symptoms. Anti-depressants can be very effective for depression but may give rise to unacceptably unpleasant side-effects and may exert only temporary improvement.

Recognizing this, many biological therapists propose drugs to facilitate psychological treatment. For example, Friedman (1988) states: 'pharmacotherapy alone is rarely sufficient to provide complete remission of PTSD. Symptom relief provided by medication enables the patient to participate more thoroughly in individual, behavioural or group psychotherapy'.

Psychodynamic treatment

There are many case reports but fewer evaluations of the effects of psychodynamic treatment for PTSD. Horowitz (1986) has postulated the clearest dynamic model for PTSD, which sees sufferers oscillating between periods of denying or strenuously resisting intrusions, and periods of domination by intrusions and repetitions of the trauma. The aim of therapy is to enable the individual to integrate the traumatic experience with his/her concept of self and the outside world.

Therapy is highly individual and reports range from lengthy to short periods of therapy. Very few psychoanalytic or psychodynamic therapists measure therapy outcome in a systematic way, rendering analysis of effectiveness very difficult. Both Horowitz *et al.* (1984) and Lindy *et al.* (1983) have shown, however, that dynamic therapy is effective with PTSD and that people treated in this way do better than those not treated at all. Although psychodynamic and analytical therapists will relate current symptoms to defence mechanisms arising out of childhood development, there is still an emphasis on helping the individual cope with the problems in the present. Imagery is an oft-used technique (Grigsby, 1987) to facilitate the survivor integrating his/her experience.

Behavioural and cognitive-behavioural treatment

Behavioural and cognitive-behavioural treatments have been developed and used successfully to help people suffering from a range of anxiety-related problems, such as phobias and obsessive-compulsive problems. During the last ten years, clinicians and researchers have applied similar techniques to PTSD. The advantages of cogniive-behavioural counselling in this area are outlined by Scott and Stradling (1992), and include problem orientation, structure, direction, specificity and an emphasis on evaluating the effectiveness or otherwise of the intervention.

Two types of therapy have predominated: those that seek to help the survivor 'process' the trauma memories and overcome his/her avoidances; and those that teach survivors additional coping skills or anxiety management techniques. Examples of the former all involve imaginal techniques and include systematic desensitization (Frank *et al.*, 1988a; Bowen and Lambert, 1989), imaginal flooding (Cooper and Clum, 1989; Keane *et al.*, 1989) and graded exposure (Richards and Rose, 1991; Richards, Lovell and Marks, 1994). An example of anxiety management techniques is stress inoculation training (SIT) (Resick *et al.*, 1988; Frank *et al.*, 1988a). Cognitive therapy (Foa *et al.*, 1991; Resick and Schnicke, 1992) integrates both 'processing' and 'coping' techniques and has been shown to be effective.

Surprisingly for a philosophy which relies on empirical research, there is still a lack of outcome studies which compare different behavioural and cognitive-behavioural techniques, and even fewer controlled studies. Most research has been carried out so far with two main groups – rape survivors (Frank *et al.*, 1988a; Foa *et al.*, 1991) and combat veterans (Cooper and Clum, 1989; Keane *et al.*, 1989). All studies are American, so cultural differences may make the application of results within the British context problematical. Numbers in most studies are small, and often waiting-list control groups are used rather than placebo techniques which would control for the effects of therapist time. Although most studies report improvement, this is often patchy, with some symptoms remaining unchanged.

The same research team who conducted the prospective trial of rape survivors described earlier (Rothbaum *et al.*, 1992) also investigated the effect of three treatments – exposure, SIT and non-directive counselling – comparing the results to a waiting-list control (Foa *et al.*, 1991). The results were as follows:

1. All three treatments reduced non-specific distress such as depression and anxiety.
2. Specific PTSD symptoms were only treated successfully by exposure or SIT, not by supportive counselling.
3. Immediately post-treatment (4½ weeks after starting), SIT produced the most consistent gains.
4. At follow-up, 3½ months later, the exposure group continued to improve, whereas the SIT group lost some of their gains. At this point, exposure was superior to SIT.

This seems to provide us with the clearest evidence that exposure to traumatic memories and avoided situations, key areas of PTSD dysfunction, is the treatment strategy of choice for PTSD. It also confirms Duckworth and Charlesworth's (1988) view that supportive counselling is only of general, not specific, use in PTSD treatment.

PTSD: SOCIAL SUPPORT

It seems commonsensical that those who have a greater range and quality of social supports will fare better than those whose use of such support is more limited. However, despite the interest in this topic from researchers, the position is far from clear. For example, after the Three Mile Island disaster, those residents with moderate to high levels of social support appeared to benefit from it (Fleming *et al.*, 1982). This is unlikely, however, to be a simple relationship. Joseph *et al.* (1993) make the point that the use of social support may be contingent on the way an individual appraises their role in an incident. They state: 'individuals who blame themselves are less likely to use coping strategies that make use of family and friends'.

In the workplace, the role of positive management gestures is seen as very positive by staff after a traumatic incident. In our own research at the Leeds Permanent (1991), 75 per cent of staff involved in robberies viewed a letter, gift or a meal out as a positive, caring gesture. Only a small minority (less than 10 per cent) would not welcome a prompt visit from a senior manager. The role of this manager is often expressed as 'defusing' – taking the heat out of the aftermath of a traumatic event by a physical reassuring presence, by using empathy and listening skills, and by taking care of the disruptive practical tasks caused by the event. It seems likely that organizational responses are at least as important as the provision of professional counselling services if recovery from the event is to take place.

PTSD: PREVENTION

Unfortunately, looking down the barrel of a gun cannot be said to be an event outside the range of usual human experience for some members of staff in banks and building societies, and indeed such experiences can produce PTSD. It is not the event *per se* which is important so much as the way the individual appraises it. Causal attributions and attributional style all seem highly important. Cognitions and cognitive style before, during and after a traumatic event will influence the development of PTSD.

It is postulated that people who deny the possibility that they will experience traumatic events are more likely to develop PTSD if such an event actually does happen to them (Resick and Schnicke, 1992). For example, a woman who believes that 'rape doesn't happen to nice women' may find it impossible to integrate a subsequent experience of rape with this prior belief, resulting in severe and prolonged post-traumatic stress. The same principle may be true of other events, including armed building-society robbery. Avoidant thinking prior to a trauma is not good preparation for the event.

Stress inoculation training (SIT) is not only a post-trauma treatment but has also been used to prepare people for forthcoming stressful events (Meichenbaum, 1985). SIT works on the principle that it is possible to inoculate oneself against future stress by previous exposure to controlled doses of the stress, a procedure analogous to biological immunization programmes. Such procedures have, of course, formed the basis of most military training for centuries. SIT takes this further, however, by its emphasis on self-understanding and psychological coping skills. Meichenbaum (1985) explains this as helping clients 'acquire sufficient knowledge, self-understanding, and coping skills to facilitate better ways of handling (un)expected stressful situations' (p. 22).

These techniques have been widely used to prepare people in stressful jobs to cope better with aspects of their work. Several studies with police officers (Novaco, 1977; Sarason *et al.*, 1979) have demonstrated the usefulness of this approach in preparatory training for violent or otherwise difficult situations. Trainees were helped to monitor their reactions during role plays of such anger-provoking or threatening situations and to identify and change inappropriate automatic thoughts.

TRAUMA IN THE WORKPLACE: PUTTING IT ALL TOGETHER

The aim of a comprehensive policy to restrict the impact of traumatic events is to *prevent* serious post-trauma reactions, to *promote* recovery after the event, and to *provide* all staff who experience such events with access to a confidential counselling service which reduces their immediate, short-term and long-term post-traumatic stress.

Figure 6.1 expresses this graphically. Immediate distress should be reduced somewhat, though not dramatically, since armed robberies, etc. should remain frightening for most people. More importantly, the rate of recovery should be speeded up and the proportion of people with long-term problems should be greatly reduced.

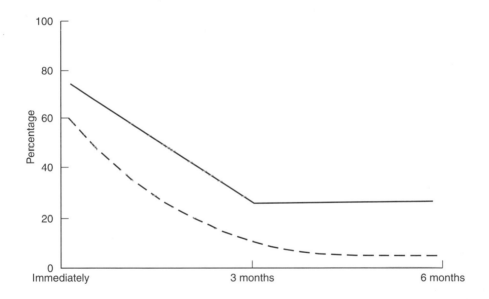

Figure 6.1 *PTSD Prevalence over time. The solid line represents the untreated post-trauma population prevalence, the broken line the aim of an integrated support programme.*

The importance of 'intersectoral' co-operation is important in the 'new public health' movement. The Health and Safety Executive's *Draft Guidance on the Prevention of Violence in Banks and Building Societies* (HSE, 1993) stresses the importance of nominating one person at a senior level in the company to co-ordinate this response. In a large company, for example, preparing for and responding to traumatic incidents such as robberies will involve the personnel, security, counselling, training and maintenance departments as well as local managers. Co-ordination is essential to ensure that the consequences of each department's actions on health are carefully considered. Multiple and conflicting messages are not conducive to an individual's speedy recovery.

Reiser and Geiger (1984) discussed this in relation to police officers. Their comments are summarized by Meichenbaum (1985), who notes that the most helpful organizational policies are those that:

> provide support and a referral network, keep postviolence interviews short, adopt a helpful rather than an adversarial attitude, communicate an awareness that victimization is traumatic for everyone, and convey the idea that unpleasant thoughts and feelings are not abnormal reactions, provide light duty assignments that allow a gradual reentry, and indicate that management and peers do care. (p. 88)

At the Leeds Permanent Building Society we therefore chose to implement an integrated system involving pre-robbery training, positive management response, the immediate availability of psychological information to victims, critical-incident stress debriefing, pro-active follow-ups, professional cognitive behavioural counselling and post-robbery psychological health monitoring. This is shown in flow-chart form in Figure 6.2.

Pre-raid training

This is the primary prevention stage, where we aimed to inoculate staff using Meichenbaum's methods by branch-based training videos of raids and positive coping strategies. Staff were also provided with a workbook to take them through the various coping strategies outlined, including basic security procedures as well as psychological methods.

Post-raid pack

In each branch a sealed emergency pack was opened immediately after a raid. It contains a procedural checklist, contact cards for the professional counsellors, and 'Coping With Robberies', a leaflet detailing some of the likely reactions to trauma and what to do in the few days post-robbery.

Immediate local management visit

Local managers, trained in 'defusing' techniques, visited as soon as possible after the raid, usually within the same day. They provided support in the immediate aftermath of the robbery and did practical things like take staff home when interviews with police were over.

Critical-incident stress debriefing (CISD)

After 48 hours we held a staff meeting of all staff at the branch, where a standard format CISD group was taken by one of the professional counsellors.

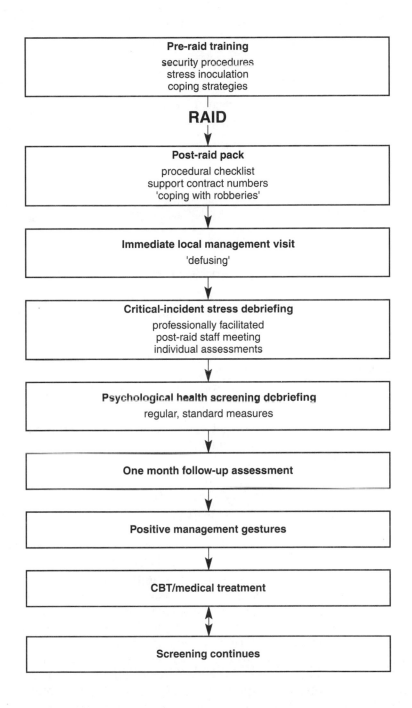

Figure 6.2 *Integrated post-raid support system*

Psychological health screening begins

Regular monitoring of psychological health commenced at this point, using standard measures such as the Impact of Events Scale (Horowitz *et al.*, 1979) and the General Health Questionnaire (Goldberg and Williams, 1988).

Positive management gestures

At some point around now, local management would write to all staff, visit again, and provide a meal out or some other gesture of support.

Follow-up

An individual follow-up interview with staff directly involved and/or disturbed by the robbery would be conducted by the debriefer to assess for PTSD or other chronic psychological distress. These interviews would be held one month after the robbery.

Cognitive-behavioural therapy and/or medical treatment

Where counselling, follow-up or the health screening measures indicated continuing problems, staff were offered more intensive cognitive-behavioural therapy. Liaison with the staff member's GP would be likely at this stage.

Screening continues

The psychological health of staff would be screened and monitored for up to two years following their involvement in a robbbery. At any time in this period, further assistance would be delivered where the screening measures indicated a problem. Furthermore, staff could of course contact the professional counsellors should they have further problems.

SUMMARY

This chapter has outlined the impact of severe stress at work on individuals exposed to incidents such as armed robbery. Reviewing the literature, it is apparent that a range of techniques are available to reduce the impact of these stresses, before, during and after the event. Putting these techniques together in a way that emphasizes health and not disease is the advantage of a comprehensive 'new public health' approach. Co-ordination, intersectoral working and 'horses for courses' counselling are the key elements in making a corporate support strategy work.

In doing this, we hope to substantially reduce the distress that a employees suffer as a consequence of robberies. We also hope to avoid the mistake of providing too much or too little counselling support at the wrong times. One by-product of a continuous health-monitoring system is to provide greater information on the best way to reduce post-traumatic stress in such at-risk occupational groups. Only by adopting such a routine evaluative strategy can we hope to base future policy on sound evidence gathered from the real experiences of employees.

REFERENCES

Alexander, P. (ed.) (1978) *William Shakespeare: The Complete Works.* London: Collins.

American Psychiatric Association (1994) *Diagnostic and Statistical Manual of Mental Disorders* (4th edn). Washington, DC: APA.

Ashton, J. and Seymour, H. (1988) *The New Public Health.* Milton Keynes: Open University Press.

Bowen, G.R. and Lambert, J.A. (1989) Systematic desensitization therapy with post-traumatic stress disorder cases. In C.R. Figley (ed.) *Trauma and its Wake.* New York: Brunner-Mazel.

Cohen, D. (1991) *Aftershock: The Psychological and Political Consequences of Disaster.* London: Paladin.

Cooper, N.A. and Clum, G.A. (1989) Imaginal flooding as a supplementary treatment for PTSD in combat veterans: A controlled study. *Behaviour Therapy*, **20**, 381–91.

Curran, P.S., Bell, P., Murray, G., Loughrey, G., Roddy, R. and Rocke, L.G. (1990) Psychological consequences of the Enniskillen bombing. *British Journal of Psychiatry*, **156**, 479–82.

Davidson, J.R.T., Hughes, D., Blazer, D.G. and George, L.K. (1991) Post-traumatic stress disorder in the community: An epidemiological study. *Psychological Medicine*, **21**, 713–21.

Department of Health (1991) *The Health of the Nation.* London: HMSO.

Duckworth, D.H. and Charlesworth, A. (1988) The human side of disaster. *Policing*, **4**, 194–210.

Dyregrov, A. (1989) Caring for helpers in disaster situations: Psychological debriefing, *Disaster Management*, **2**, 25–30.

Fleming, R., Baum, A., Gisriel, M.M. and Gatchel, R.A. (1982) Mediating influences of social support on stress at Three Mile Island. *Journal of Human Stress*, **8**, 14–22.

Foa, E.B., Rothbaum, B.O., Riggs, D.S. and Murdock, T.B. (1991) Treatment of post traumatic stress disorder in rape victims: A comparison between cognitive-behavioural procedures and counselling, *Journal of Consulting and Clinical Psychology*, **59**, 715–23.

Frank, E., Anderson, B., Stewart, B.D., Dancu, C., Hughes, C. and West, D. (1988) Efficacy of cognitive-behaviour therapy and systematic desensitization in the treatment of rape trauma. *Behaviour Therapy*, **19**, 403–20.

Frank, J.B., Kosten, T.R., Giller, E.L. and Dan, E. (1988) A randomized clinical trial of phenalzine and imiprimine for post-traumatic stress disorder. *American Journal of Psychiatry*, **145**, 1289–91.

Friedman, M.J. (1988) Towards rational pharmacotherapy for post-traumatic stress disorder: An interim report. *American Journal of Psychiatry*, **145**, 281–5.

Goldberg, D. and Williams, P. (1988) *A User's Guide to the General Health Questionnaire*. Windsor: NFER-Nelson.

Grigsby, J.P. (1987) The use of imagery in the treatment of post-traumatic stress disorder. *Journal of Nervous and Mental Disease*, **175**, 55–9.

Health and Safety Executive (1993) *Draft Guidance on the Prevention of Violence to Staff in Banks and Building Societies*. London: HSE.

Helzer, J.E., Robbins, L.N. and McEvoy, L. (1987) Post-traumatic stress disorder in the general population: Findings from the epidemiological catchment area survey. *New England Journal of Medicine*, **317**, 1630–4.

Home Office (1991) *Disasters: Planning for a Caring Response*. London: HMSO.

Hodgkinson, P.E. and Stewart, M. (1991) *Coping with Catastrophe: A Handbook of Disaster Management*. London: Routledge.

Horowitz, M.J. (1986) *Stress Response Syndromes*. New York: Jason Aronson.

Horowitz, M., Wilner, N. and Alvarez, W. (1979) Impact of event scale: A measure of subjective stress. *Psychosomatic Medicine*, **41**, 209–18.

Horowitz, M.J., Marmar, C., Weiss, D.S., Dewitt, K.N. and Rosenbaum, R. (1984) Brief psychotherapy of bereavement reactions: The relationship of process to outcome. *Archives of General Psychiatry*, **41**, 438–48.

Jacobson, B., Smith, A. and Whitehead, M. (1991) *The Nation's Health: A Strategy for the 1990s*. London: King's Fund.

Joseph, S., Yule, W. and Williams, R. (1993) Post-traumatic stress: Attributional aspects. *Journal of Traumatic Stress*, **6**, 501–13.

Keane, T.M., Fairbank, J.A., Caddell, J.M. and Zimmering, R.T. (1989) Implosive (flooding) therapy reduces symptoms of PTSD in Vietnam combat veterans. *Behaviour Therapy*, **20**, 245–60.

Kolb, L.C. (1987) A neuropsychological hypothesis explaining post-traumatic stress disorders. *American Journal of Psychiatry*, **144**, 989–95.

Lane, D.A. (1991) Psychological aspects of disaster: Issues for the 1990s. *British Journal of Guidance and Counselling*, **19**, 31–43.

Leeds Permanent Building Society (1991) Staff research on trauma in the workplace (unpublished survey report).

Lindy, J.D., Green, B.L., Grace, M. and Titchener, J. (1983) Psychotherapy with survivors of the Beverly Hills Supper Club fire. *American Journal of Psychotherapy*, 37, 593–610.

Meichenbaum, D. (1985) *Stress Inoculation Training*. New York: Pergamon Press.

Novaco, R. (1977) A stress inoculation approach to anger management in the training of law enforcement officers. *American Journal of Community Psychology*, 5, 327–46.

Noy, S., Levy, R. and Solomon, Z. (1984) Mental health care in the Lebanon War, 1982. *Israel Journal of Medical Sciences*, 20, 361.

Raphael, B. (1986) *When Disaster Strikes: A Handbook for the Caring Professions*. London: Hutchinson.

Reiser, M. and Geiger, S. (1984) Police officer as victim. *Professional Psychology: Research and Practice*, 15, 315–23.

Reist, C., Kauffmann, C.D. and Haier, R.J. (1989) A controlled trial of desimipramine in 18 men with post-traumatic stress disorder. *American Journal of Psychiatry*, 146, 513–16.

Resick, P.A. and Schnicke, M.K. (1992) Cognitive processing therapy for sexual assault victims. *Journal of Consulting and Clinical Psychology*, 60, 748–56.

Resick, P.A., Jordan, C.G., Girrelli, S.A., Hutter, C.K. and Marhoefer-Dvorack, S. (1988) A comparative outcome study of behavioural group therapy for sexual assault victims. *Behaviour Therapy*, 19, 385–401.

Richards, D.A. and Deale, A. (1990) The effect of a raid video on Society staff. Unpublished report for the Nationwide Building Society.

Richards, D.A. and Rose, J.S. (1991) Exposure therapy for post-traumatic stress disorder: Four case studies. *British Journal of Psychiatry*, 158, 836–40.

Richards, D.A., Lovell, K. and Marks, I.M. (1994) Post-traumatic stress disorder: Evaluation of a behavioural treatment programme. *Journal of Traumatic Stress*, 7(4), 669–80.

Rothbaum, B.O., Foa, E.B., Riggs, D.S., Murdock, T. and Walsh, W. (1992) A prospective examination of post-traumatic stress disorder in rape victims. *Journal of Traumatic Stress*, 5, 455–75.

Sarason, I., Johnson, J., Berberich, J. and Siegel, J. (1979) Helping police officers to cope with stress: A cognitive-behavioural approach. *American Journal of Community Psychology*, 7, 593–603.

Scott, M.J. and Stradling, S.G. (1992) *Counselling for Post-Traumatic Stress Disorder*. London: Sage.

Solomon, Z. (1989) A three year prospective study of post-traumatic stress disorder in Israeli combat veterans. *Journal of Traumatic Stress*, 2, 59–73.

Thompson, J. (1993) Psychotherapy: Debriefing and CEASE – three treatment trials for post-trauma reactions. Paper presented at Research Foundations for Psychotherapy Services, Oxford, September.

Van der Kolk, B.A. (1987) The drug treatment of post-traumatic stress disorder. *Journal of Affective Disorders*, **13**, 203–13.

Van der Kolk, B.A., Greenberg, M.S., Boyd, H. and Krystal, J. (1985) Inescapable shock, neurotransmitters and addiction to trauma: Towards a psychobiology of post-traumatic stress. *Biological Psychiatry*, **20**, 314–25.

CHAPTER 7

Stress Management Interventions in the Workplace: Stress Counselling and Stress Audits

Cary L. Cooper and Sue Cartwright

Within the field of stress management intervention, there have been substantial disagreements on the 'right' approach. Some argue for counselling and stress management training, while others argue for more substantive organizational change through stress audits. It is argued that both are important in meeting the needs of individuals and organizations.

INTRODUCTION

The costs of occupational stress to business and industry in monetary terms have become increasingly well documented. Annually, US industry loses approximately 550 million working days due to absenteeism. It is estimated (Elkin and Rosch, 1990) that 54 per cent of these absences are in some way stress-related. Recent figures released by the Confederation of British Industry (Sigman, 1992) calculate that in the UK, 360 million working days are lost annually through sickness, at a cost to organizations of £8 billion. Again, it is estimated by the Health and Safety Executive that at least half of these lost days relate to stress-related absence. In addition to the direct costs of sickness absence, labour turnover and poor productivity, there is an indirect cost about to enter the UK scene: stress-related workers' compensation.

For many years now, employees in the USA have been litigating against their employers for job-related stress or what they term 'cumulative trauma' in the workplace. For example, in California, the stress-related compensation claims for psychiatric injury now total over 3,000 a year, since the California Supreme Court upheld its first stress disability case in the early 1970s. The California Labour Code now states specifically that workers' compensation is allowable for disability or illness caused by 'repetitive mentally or physically traumatic activities extending over a period of time, the combined effect of which causes any disability or need for medical treatment'. The first 'cumulative trauma' or stress at work cases are currently being deliberated by the High Court in the UK, and many more cases are in the lower courts. The UK courts are likely, therefore, to accept workers' compensation for 'stress caused by work' in the near future.

In addition to this negative motivation, in the last few years there has been an explosion of health promotion or 'wellness' programmes in US and UK industry. Such activities as exercise, stress management training, smoking cessation and counselling are being encouraged by virtually every medium available – radio, TV, magazines, books – and are taking place not only in the home, schools, etc. but also in the workplace.

A MODEL OF STRESS MANAGEMENT INTERVENTIONS

Given that stress management at the worksite may be a valuable component of a health promotion programme and important in the avoidance of litigation, it follows that the availability of these programmes will continue to increase in the future. It is also apparent that employers, providers and researchers need to broaden their conceptualization of the focus of stress management interventions and the potential range of outcomes for these programmes. This is necessary because activities aimed solely at individuals' reactions to stressful circumstances, and not also targeted at modifying the circumstances themselves, will not be sufficient to avoid the negative legal ramifications just discussed. Expanding the focus of inquiry also provides a clearer picture of the phenomena under study, offers more avenues for intervention and evaluation, and improves the chances for behaviour change.

An example of this expansion of perspective was highlighted by DeFrank and Cooper (1987) in a scheme for viewing the various levels of stress management interventions and outcomes (Table 7.1). Three levels are postulated, focusing on the individual, the individual/organizational interface, and the organization. With regard to interventions, the listing contains those factors which could serve as the target for a stress management intervention programme. These include a set of techniques aimed at the individual, such as relaxation, biofeedback and meditation which target physical concomitants of stress such as muscle tension or blood pressure. Other coping strategies such as cognitive restructuring and time management reflect attempts to alter the ways in which people structure and organize their worlds. Exercise has been noted to improve both physical endurance and mood states, and Employee Assistance Programmes typically provide counselling and referral for employee problems. The individual outcomes that could be used to assess the impacts of these procedures range from the biochemical and physical (e.g. catecholamines, blood pressure, muscle tension) to the psychological (e.g. moods, life satisfaction), with some outcomes in the middle of this range (e.g. psychosomatic complaints such as headaches, nausea, sweating palms, dizziness). This category, in sum, places attention specifically on the person, and the ways in which he/she responds to and copes with stress, regardless of the source of stress.

The next level encompasses the interface between the individual and the organization, emphasizing here targets of interventions rather than the techniques themselves, as the latter are not well developed for this kind of interaction. These factors are often cited as major products of stress in the workplace. For example, conflict among varied roles and ambiguity over the content and responsibilities of

Table 7.1 *Levels of stress management interventions and outcomes*

Interventions	Outcomes
Focus on individual	*Focus on individual*
Relaxation techniques	Mood states (depression, anxiety)
Cognitive coping strategies	Psychosomatic complaints
Biofeedback	Subjectively experienced stress
Meditation	Physiological parameters (blood
Exercise	pressure, catecholamines,
Employee Assistance Programmes (EAPs)	muscle tension) sleep
Time management	disturbances
	Life satisfaction
Focus on individual/organizational	*Focus on individual/organizational*
interface	*interface*
Relationships at work	Job stress
Person environment fit	Job satisfaction
Role issues	Burnout
Participation and autonomy	Productivity and performance
	Absenteeism
	Turnover
	Health care utilization and claims
Focus on organization	*Focus on organization*
Organizational structure	Productivity
Selection and placement	Turnover
Training	Absenteeism
Physical and environmental characteristics	Health care claims
of job	Recruitment/retention success
Health concerns and resources	
Job rotation	

Source: DeFrank and Cooper, 1987

these roles may lead to the increased job stress and decreased job satisfaction (Van Sell *et al.*, 1981; Fisher and Gitelson, 1983). Similarly, a lack of fit between the objective and subjective characteristics of an environment and the corresponding aspects of an individual may produce significant stress and strain (Caplan, 1983; Harrison, 1985). The outcome variables for this category, as at the individual focus level, include a range of alternatives. Some are measured by self-report indices such as job stress and satisfaction, and burnout. Other variables are considerably more objective in nature, including absenteeism, turnover and health care claims. Productivity may or may not be included in this latter category, as it may be easy to determine for some workers (e.g. assembly-line workers) and more difficult to estimate for others (e.g. managers).

The third level of interventions and outcomes focuses on the organization as the target for stress management programmes. This list suggests some of the areas in which organizational environment, structure and policies may produce stress for employees. For example, such physical characteristics of the job as excessive heat and noise may produce strain among workers and increase the probability of accidents (Bell and Greene, 1982; Cohen and Weinstein, 1982). Shift schedule, a structural aspect of work, can engender a significant level of physical and mental discomfort if not ordered correctly (Tasto and Colligan, 1978). In addition, policies relating to job training and availability of health care are likely to have an impact on the work performance and satisfaction of employees. A number of the relevant outcomes have been mentioned above, but in this context they are viewed at the organizational rather than the individual level. Also, many of these organizational issues will influence the quality of employees that can be recruited and the ability to retain employees once they are hired.

It should be noted that there is a degree of unavoidable overlap in this ordering, as the levels are not independent of each other. For example, the impact of the physical characteristics of the job will be modified to some extent by the individual's perception of them. On the other hand, the availability of time to mediate may be a function of environmental demands. Despite these interrelationships, these three categories of interventions provide a useful classification method that can be applied to outcomes as well. This approach extends our attention to variables that we might not have considered previously as relevant to determining the effect of a stress management programme. However, a broadened range of interventions requires a similarly expanded outcome list, and the impact of a particular intervention should be assessed at a variety of levels to determine its true importance. Note also that overlap occurs quite explicitly among these outcome measures, as productivity, turnover, absenteeism and health care claims all appear twice. These are factors that reflect the interaction between person and environment, and also have significant implications for organizational functioning.

From the above model we can see that interventions are needed at all levels, from the individual to the corporate. At present, most interventions take place at the individual level or in training, with few targeted toward minimizing the organizational stressors or providing in-depth stress counselling. What is needed is more of both of the latter: that is, stress auditing to identify sources of workplace stress, so that organizations can adequately and appropriately intervene; and more stress counselling, so that individuals with problems either related or unrelated to the workplace can get help and support in resolving them.

STRESS COUNSELLING AT WORK

An example of 'good practice' in terms of stress counselling can be found in the UK Post Office experiment (some of the material in this section is drawn from Allison *et al.*, 1989, and Sadri *et al.*, 1989, and more details of this project can be found there). The idea of a specialist counselling facility within the Post Office was formulated by the then chief medical officer, Dr Michael McDonald. Stress had been identified as an organizational problem in the 1970s, when stress factors were found to be the second highest reason for medical retirement after muscular skeletal illnesses. In

1984, Dr McDonald recommended the setting up of a working party to identify the needs of Post Office staff in respect of specialist counselling on stress. Membership of the working group was selected in order to provide an appropriate balance of view between the business specialist functions and its line managers, while at the same time ensuring representation from each of the three hierarchical administrative levels of the business. The group, therefore, included a range of opinion and experience in both the counselling and health education fields, as well as in the operation and resourcing of the Post Office as a whole.

The report acknowledged that the Post Office already offered basic counselling support to employees, through their nursing and welfare officers (available to be seen by employees with problems). But the specialist role was recommended to deal with more complex and deep-seated psychological problems, of the kind which previously, perhaps, would have been referred outside the Post Office to some other agency. It was also assumed that, unlike external specialists, in-house specialist counsellors would have the benefit of a broad knowledge of the postal business and methods, and would be better able to understand and directly help employees, particularly where the problem was work-related. Furthermore, it was felt that the external agencies were so 'client-oriented' that they knew less about the organization-behaviour aspects of workplace stress.

One other important aspect of the role was that the specialist counsellors might also be able to identify if any Post Office structures, policies or practices were causing psychological problems among employees. They would then be able to brief senior management about those aspects of the business operations which were causing psychological difficulties, without identifying individuals or breaching confidentiality. Furthermore, they might contribute in the future to the formulation of business practices in a way that would minimize the stressful impact on staff. In practice this proved difficult, given the demands on the counselling service.

An early decision was to locate the counsellors within the Post Office's occupational health service. While this is not surprising, given that the impetus for specialist counselling came from members of the occupational health service, it did imply particular organizational consequences. First, the concept of health (despite the efforts of health educationalists) often implies illness. For example, to many people a health clinic is perceived as a doctor's surgery and is only visited during periods of illness. Following from this, one would expect that within an occupational health setting a proportion of the caseload would be chronic conditions involving long-term sickness absence and/or a last resort before medical retirement. Secondly, location within the occupational health service implied certain professional ethics governing conduct and confidentiality. Indeed, it is very difficult to envisage any other department in a commercial organization which could offer similar 'taken for granted' assumptions. In practice, both these points proved to be the case.

From the outset, the Post Office counselling service was envisaged as an open-access service; therefore, referrals were received from all quarters. Obviously, by virtue of the fact that counselling was located in occupational health, there was a tendency for a large number of referrals to emanate from this quarter. However, ongoing publicity such as letters to employees, articles in the house magazine and presentations to management groups served to promote other avenues. A breakdown of sources of referral during the first 22 months of the project revealed that the bulk were from occupational health (40%), self-referral (31.5%) and welfare (19%), with the remaining 9.5% coming from such areas as management, personnel and trade unions.

At the outset, counsellors expected a hesitant start to the project. They believed that it would take some six to nine months to gain a foothold in the organization, and build some degree of credibility among the various interest groups. However, these assumptions proved incorrect. Setting aside the first month, which was spent in induction, the caseload for the first 22 months totalled 353. Furthermore, this was spread across the entire organization, including cleaners, postmen/women, postal officers and executives, technical engineers and senior staff. As one might anticipate, problems do not respect organizational positions or boundaries.

The largest cluster of client problems were in the broad category of mental health and stress issues, which represented 46% of the caseload. These clients were normally suffering from anxiety and/or depression. Occasionally single or multiple causes became evident, but often not. Of the remaining 54% of referrals, the second most significant group was that surrounding 'relationship' problems (24%), with the majority focusing on marital difficulties. Other areas included alcoholism and addictions, bereavement, assault and physical illness or disability.

A main feature of the stress counselling programme in the Post Office was its evaluation. It was found that clients' psychological well-being improved at the completion of counselling (Cooper and Sadri, 1991). Clients were less anxious, less depressed, suffered from fewer psychosomatic symptoms of stress and had a higher level of self-esteem. Clients also showed significant changes on a number of behavioural items. After counselling, the client group used less of the following health behaviours: drink coffee/coke or eat frequently; smoke; and use alcohol to cope with events. Respondents also indicated that they felt less guilty about drinking. On the other hand, they used more of the following measures to relax at work: relaxation techniques (e.g. meditation or yoga); informal relaxation techniques (e.g. deep breathing or imagining pleasant scenes); exercise; leaving work area and going somewhere (e.g. lunching away from the organization, taking time out); and using humour. Clients also found more time to relax and 'wind down' after work. In addition, counselling had an impact on substantially reducing sickness absence events and days. It was also found, however, that although counselling had an effect on the mental well-being and sickness absence of those counselled, it had little impact on their level of job satisfaction or organizational commitment. This is not surprising, since counselling is attempting to improve an individual's coping capabilities: why, therefore, should we expect this to affect the nature of a specific job or a substantive feature of an organization (i.e. its management style or communication structure)?

WORKPLACE STRESS AUDITS

Workplace stress counselling, and even stress management training (e.g. time management, relaxation training, cognitive skill development), has an important part to play in extending the individual's psychological and physical resources. But its role is essentially one of 'damage limitation', often addressing the *consequences* rather than the *sources* of stress which may be inherent in the organization's structure or culture.

Elkin and Rosch (1990) summarize a useful range of possible organization-directed strategies to reduce stress:

- redesign the task;
- redesign the work environment;
- establish flexible work schedules;
- encourage participative management;
- include the employee in career development;
- analyse work roles and establish goals;
- provide social support and feedback;
- build cohesive teams;
- establish fair employment policies;
- share the rewards.

Many of these strategies are directed at increasing employee participation. Indirectly, they are often a vehicle for culture change, moving the organization towards a more open and 'employee empowered' culture. Implementation of these, however, is often expensive, potentially disruptive and may result in major restructuring. Few organizations would be prepared to commit themselves to extensive change programmes without justification of their necessity and/or a baseline measure by which to evaluate their effectiveness. In the same way that different stressors are responsible for different outcomes (Cooper *et al.*, 1988a), the potential sources of stress have been shown to vary between different occupational groups. For example, money-handling and the risk of personal assault was found to be a major occupational stressor amongst bus drivers in the UK transport industry (Duffy and McGoldrick, 1990), whereas the major source of stress for UK income tax officers was autocratic management style and lack of consultation (Cooper and Roden, 1985). Furthermore, differences have been found between institutions and organizations in the same industry or business sector (Kahn and Cooper, 1993), and between different subcultures and status groups within the same organization (Cooper and Bramwell, 1992). Consequently, the type of action required by an organization to reduce or eliminate workplace stressors will vary according to the kinds of stressors operating, the level of coping skills of those involved and the culture of the organization. In the samples given above, stress reduction might suggest a possible ergonomic solution in the case of bus drivers, whereas a change in management style which leads to increased employee participation is more likely to reduce the stress experienced by income tax officers.

What is needed, therefore, are regular and detailed organizational *stress audits*, sampling different jobs, departments and sections of the workforce (e.g. women *v.* men, ethnic minorities, new recruits, graduates, shopfloor *v.* managerial employees, etc.). Psychometric instruments (e.g. Occupational Stress-Indicators or OSI) are now available to carry out this task and more will be available in the near future.

The OSI (Cooper *et al.*, 1988b) or other similar instruments provide an effective means whereby organizations can regularly audit and monitor organizational health, and be proactive in stress reduction. In addition, such audits can be used to provide a baseline measure, whereby stress reduction techniques can be evaluated. The use of audits could be extended to ascertain employee attitudes and perceived needs for stress management training or counselling, to provide valuable information regarding the likely 'take up' rates of such programmes before any expenditure is incurred.

CONCLUSION

Occupational stress is likely to continue to present a major threat to the financial health and profitability of organizations. Growing health and safety legislation, escalating insurance costs and fear of litigation will increasingly force organizations to take a more responsible attitude towards stress reduction. Counselling and stress management training have useful roles to play, but organizational preoccupation with the *outcome* of the stress process has tended to detract from the more proactive approach of addressing the *source* or causal factors in the stress process (i.e. the 'front end' issues). Rather than focusing exclusively on what the organization can *provide* for the employee to help them cope with stress more effectively, organizations would be well advised to consider what the organization can *do* to eliminate or reduce workplace stressors (Cartwright and Cooper, 1994).

REFERENCES

Allison, T., Cooper, C.L. and Reynolds, P. (1989) Stress counselling in the workplace. *The Psychologist*, **2**, 384–8.

Bell, P.A. and Greene, T.C. (1982) Thermal stress: Physiological, comfort performance, and social effects of hot and cold environments. In G.W. Evans (ed.), *Environmental Stress*, Cambridge: Cambridge University Press.

Caplan, R.D. (1983) Person–environment fit: Past, present and future. In C.L. Cooper (ed.), *Stress Research: Issues for the Eighties*. Chichester: Wiley.

Cartwright, S. and Cooper, C.L. (1994) Healthy mind; healthy organization – a proactive approach to occupational stress. *Human Relations*, **47**(4), 455–71.

Cohen, S. and Weinstein, N. (1982) Nonauditory effects of noise on behaviour and health. In G.W. Evans (ed.), *Environmental Stress*. Cambridge: Cambridge University Press.

Cooper, C.L. and Bramwell, S. (1992) A comparative analysis of occupational stress in managerial and shopfloor workers in the brewing industry: Mental health, job satisfaction and sickness. *Work and Stress*, **6**, 127–38.

Cooper, C.L. and Roden, J. (1985) Mental health and satisfaction among tax officers. *Social Science and Medicine*, **21**, 747–51.

Cooper, C.L. and Sadri, G. (1991) The impact of stress counselling at work. *Journal of Social Behavior and Personality*, **6**, 411–23.

Cooper, C.L., Cooper, R.D. and Eaker, L. (1988a) *Living with Stress.* London: Penguin Books.

Cooper, C.L., Sloan, S. and Williams, S. (1988b) *Occupational Stress Indicator: Management Guide.* Windsor: NFER-Nelson.

DeFrank, R.S. and Cooper, C.L. (1987) Worksite stress management interventions: Their effectiveness and conceptualization. *Journal of Managerial Psychology*, **2**, 40–50.

Duffy, C.A. and McGoldrick, A. (1990) Stress and the bus driver in the UK transport industry. *Work and Stress*, **4**, 17–27.

Elkin, A.J. and Rosch, P.J. (1990) Promoting mental health at work. *Occupational Medicine State of the Art Review*, **5**, 739–54.

Fisher, C.D. and Gitelson, R. (1983) A meta-analysis of the correlates of role conflict and ambiguity. *Journal of Applied Psychology*, **68**, 320–33.

Harrison, R.V. (1985) The person–environment fit model and the study of job stress. In T.A. Beehr and R.S. Bhagat (eds), *Human Stress and Cognition in Organizations: An Integrated Perspective.* New York: Wiley.

Kahn, H. and Cooper, C.L. (1993) *Stress in the Dealing Room.* London: Routledge.

Sadri, G., Cooper, C.L. and Allison, T. (1989) A Post Office initiative to stamp out stress. *Personnel Management*, August, 40–5.

Sigman, A. (1992) The state of corporate health care. *Personnel Management*, February, 24–31.

Tasto, D.L. and Colligan, M.J. (1978) Health consequences of shift work. Stanford Research Institute Technical Report, Project URU-4426, Menlo Park, CA.

Van Sell, M., Brief, A.P. and Schuler, R.S. (1981) Role conflict and ambiguity: Integration of the literature and directions for future research. *Human Relations*, **34**, 43–71.

PART FOUR

Stress Management: Research, Issues and Methodology

CHAPTER 8

Stress Management Approaches to the Prevention of Coronary Heart Disease

Paul Bennett and Douglas Carroll

This chapter reviews evidence for the effectiveness of stress management techniques in reducing three risk factors for coronary heart disease: Type A behaviour, raised serum cholesterol and hypertension. Preliminary evidence suggests that such interventions not only reduce individual risk factors, they can also reduce mortality and morbidity to CHD. Consideration now has to be given to the most effective system of delivery of such interventions.

INTRODUCTION

Coronary heart disease (CHD) remains one of the major causes of premature death in Britain (Wells, 1987). It is also one of the diseases most closely linked to lifestyle and, as such, risk may be manipulated by altering lifestyle variables. As a result, clinical and health psychologists are increasingly becoming involved with clients identified as at high risk of developing CHD, either formally as part of a preventive programme (e.g. Bennett *et al.*, 1989) or informally through contacts with general practitioners, physicians and so on. This chapter examines a number of stress management approaches applicable to such individuals, focusing on one behavioural (Type A behaviour: TAB) and two biological (raised serum cholesterol and hypertension) risk factors. It is important to note that such interventions form only a subset of those appropriate to the prevention of CHD. Other forms of intervention, either alone or in conjunction with stress management techniques, may more usefully be considered for those at risk for example from obesity, smoking or sedentary lifestyle. Nevertheless, stress management procedures form a significant preventive intervention, and are the focus of the present chapter.

TYPE A BEHAVIOUR

Type A behaviour remains the only behaviourally defined risk factor for CHD (Review Panel on Coronary-Prone Behavior and Coronary Heart Disease, 1981).

Although its status is now controversial, the majority of prospective epidemiological studies in healthy subjects show TAB independently to predict CHD; it is generally methodologically weaker studies of re-infarction and correlational studies of TAB and degree of atherosclerosis as determined by angiography that have provided conflicting evidence (Haynes and Mathews, 1988). Nevertheless, future research will probably focus on hostility and anger as major precursors of heart disease, and allocate a less central role to other component behaviours such as time urgency and competitiveness (Bennett and Carroll, 1989; Williams and Barefoot, 1988).

Intervention research needs to show both that TAB can be modified and that such changes are related to reduced morbidity for CHD. Such evidence can be gained most easily from intervention studies in post-myocardial infarction patients, where further infarcts are statistically more probable over a relatively short period than in healthy individuals. The most extensive of such studies yet undertaken, the Recurrent Coronary Prevention Project (RCPP; Friedman et al., 1986), compared the effectiveness of group cardiac counselling v. cardiac counselling combined with TAB modification in over 800 subjects who had an infarction at least six months previously and who did not smoke. Each group met at increasing intervals for the 4½-year life of the project. Cardiac counselling consisted primarily of discussions aimed at increasing adherence to prescribed dietary, exercise and drug regimes. Type A counselling used a wide variety of cognitive and behavioural techniques (including relaxation, cognitive restructuring and graded behavioural assignments) to modify TAB. These are described in some detail in Thoresen et al. (1982) and Friedman and Ulmer (1984). Assessments were made yearly for the first three years, and at 4½ years. At each comparison, significantly greater reductions in TAB were found on self-report, spouse ratings and observed TAB on the Videotaped Structured Interview (VSI; Friedman and Powell, 1984) in the combined counselling group. Using an intention to treat analysis, by the final assessment cumulative total re-infarction was virtually halved in the combined treatment group (12.9 v. 21.2 per cent). Perhaps even more persuasively, participants in either group who reported significant behavioural change at the end of the first year subsequently had significantly fewer recurrences in the remaining 3½ years than those who failed to do so.

Other studies (e.g. Oldenburg et al., 1985; Rahe et al., 1973) also suggest that psychological intervention may reduce the risk of re-infarction or further hospitalization, but the study designs do not allow such risk reduction to be attributable to changes in TAB.

Whilst there are more reports of interventions to modify TAB in healthy (usually male) populations, these have been compromised by a primary failure to measure indices of CHD. Other methodological weaknesses include low subject numbers (Hart, 1984; Jenni and Wollersheim, 1979), limited or no follow-up (Gill et al., 1985; Jenni and Wollersheim, 1979; Levenkron et al., 1983; Roskies et al., 1986; Suinn and Bloom, 1978), failure to measure directly Type A behaviour (Roskies et al., 1979), or lack of control groups (Razin et al., 1986–7). Despite their weaknesses, these studies consistently show TAB to be modifiable, at least in the short term, through the use of cognitive-behavioural techniques in populations as diverse as students (Thurman, 1983), business executives (Roskies et al., 1986), and senior army officers (Gill et al., 1985).

One of the few studies to follow up subjects, after one year, was conducted by Thurman (1985a, b). Subjects were randomly allocated to either Rational Emotive Therapy (RET; Ellis, 1974) and anger management training (Novaco, 1978) alone or in combination with brief assertiveness training, or an information only condition. Following an eight-week intervention, TAB as measured by the Bortner Rating Scale (BRS; Bortner, 1969) and Jenkins Activity Survey (JAS; Jenkins et al., 1979), Type A irrational beliefs, trait anger (Spielberger et al., 1983) and hostility (Cook and Medley, 1954) were significantly reduced in the intervention groups only. Collateral reports indicated changes on BRS Type A scores, but not trait anger. By one-year follow-up, there was a continued superiority of the two interventions on measures of JAS Type A, Type A irrational beliefs, hostility, and collateral BRS scores. Average JAS scores fell from the 85th and 90th centiles to the 65th percentile by one-year follow-up.

Two other studies are noteworthy, as they involve reasonably large subject numbers. Gill et al. (1985) applied the intervention approach used in the RCCP in an attempt to reduce TAB in senior army officers attending the US Army War College, preparing for high-level commands. Over 100 volunteers were randomly assigned to active intervention or a no-treatment control, with intervention subjects meeting in small groups regularly during the course of the eight-month study. By the end of the study, reductions in TAB (as well as free-floating hostility and time urgency) were greater for intervention subjects than controls on the VSI and RCCP self- and spouse-completed Type A ratings. Encouragingly, these changes did not detract from peer ratings of leadership potential. However, they did develop during a period of relatively stress-free learning and self-appraisal, and the failure to monitor subjects after they returned to posts of responsibility is regrettable. Roskies et al. (1986) randomly assigned subjects to one of three group interventions: cognitive behavioural stress management (including anger-hostility control through the use of relaxation, communication training, cognitive restructuring, stress inoculation and problem-solving), aerobic exercise (jogging), and weight training. Stress management aimed at enhancing general coping abilities rather than modifying TAB per se, and is fully described in Roskies (1987). Between 20 and 30 sessions were conducted for each group over a 10-week period. Following intervention, changes in Structured Interview (Rosenman, 1978) Type A scores differed according to condition; stress management (13 to 23 per cent reductions from initial values), weight training (0 to 12 per cent reductions), and aerobic exercise (no change). Statistically greater reductions in component scores of the SI (Dembroski et al., 1978), including hostility, were also found in the stress mangement intervention.

A number of conclusions can be drawn from these studies. Type A behaviour is modifiable – although the durability of behavioural change, at least in healthy individuals, remains to be determined. Further, at least in post-infarction patients, these changes are associated with reductions in morbidity and mortality from CHD. Two differing intervention approaches can be differentiated in the studies to date – the learning and practice of Type B behaviours (e.g. Friedman et al., 1986) and the learning of generalized coping skills (e.g. Roskies et al., 1986).

Two differing underlying treatment philosophies can also be identified. The first, again exemplified by the RCCP, requires subjects to accept a radical move toward the positive attribution of Type B qualities. The second (e.g. Hart, 1984; Jenni and Wollersheim, 1979) uses Type B 'skills' as a means of gaining Type A 'ends'. Whilst the latter approach may be more attractive to CHD-free individuals, the long-term implications of such an approach are unclear. Maintenance of behavioural change may require more radical lifestyle appraisals (Price, 1988). Despite the pre-eminence of the protracted intervention of the RCCP, length of intervention may not be a crucial outcome variable (Nunes *et al.*, 1987), at least in the immediate effects of intervention, although maintenance of behaviour change may require longer-term booster sessions. Some consideration needs to be given to the most appropriate population to target such an approach. A post-myocardial infarction (MI) population would seem an excellent target population, as they are likely to be highly motivated and are at risk of further infarction. Intervention in CHD-free individuals may be optimal when other markers of CHD, such as hypertension or raised serum cholesterol, are identified and manageable following similar procedures.

RAISED SERUM CHOLESTEROL

Levels of serum cholesterol above 5.2 mmol/litre (hypercholesterolaemia) significantly raise an individual's risk of developing CHD (e.g. Study Group of the European Atherosclerosis Society, 1987). Hypercholesterolaemia is in fact a group of disorders. The most common forms are related to increased levels of low-density lipoproteins (LDLs) or very low-density lipoproteins (VLDLs), and, at least in part, are amenable to non-pharmacological interventions. Tradition, and efficacy (but see for example Mitchell, 1984; Sanders, 1987), have given dietary intervention pre-eminence in the field.

While TAB may be an independent pathogenic factor in CHD, it has also been associated with raised total serum and LDL cholesterol (Blumenthal *et al.*, 1978; Lovallo and Pishkin, 1980; Rosenman *et al.*, 1975). This finding is not universal, however, both in middle-aged men (Gallacher *et al.*, 1988) and young adults (McCranie *et al.*, 1981). Life stress has also been associated with increases in serum cholesterol and LDL levels (e.g. Francis, 1979; Trevisan *et al.*, 1983). Such findings suggest that another method of reducing serum cholesterol may be through the use of stress management techniques and the modification of TAB.

Unfortunately, most studies providing evidence concerning the effectiveness of such interventions have not used serum cholesterol levels as a primary outcome measure and have failed to control other relevant variables, such as exercise and diet (e.g. Gill *et al.*, 1985; Jenni and Wollersheim, 1979; Suinn and Bloom, 1978). They have also focused on subjects having normal to high-normal serum cholesterol levels, thus reducing the possible effect size of any intervention, and used low subject numbers (e.g. Curtis, 1974; Jenni and Wollersheim, 1979; Levenkron *et al.*, 1983; Suinn, 1975; Suinn and Bloom, 1978). Thus, it is perhaps not surprising that while some reductions in cholesterol have been found following RET (Jenni and Wollersheim, 1979) and cognitive-behavioural modification of TAB (Curtis, 1974), they have failed to achieve statistical significance. More difficult to explain are studies in which cholesterol levels have increased following stress management

(Jenni and Wollersheim, 1979; Levenkron *et al.*, 1983; Suinn and Bloom, 1978) or psychotherapy (Levenkron *et al.*, 1983). While the Levenkron *et al.* study did result in significant behavioural change following intervention, the others found little behavioural change, making the effect of such changes on serum cholesterol far from clear.

Only three studies of interventions to modify TAB have attempted even minimal control over diet or other related factors. Roskies *et al.* (1978) specifically requested subjects not to alter their diet, smoking or exercise patterns during a study comparing a 14-week psychotherapy intervention with training and *in vivo* practice of progressive muscle relaxation. All subjects were initially rated as Type A1 on the SI (Rosenman, 1978). Immediately post-intervention both the psychotherapy and relaxation group had significantly reduced serum cholesterol levels. At six-month follow-up (Roskies *et al.*, 1979), these changes were maintained in the relaxation group but not in the psychotherapy condition. Type A behaviour was not directly measured, so the relationship between behavioural and physiological change cannot be gauged. Suinn (1975) followed post-MI patients during either a brief (five-session) stress management programme or a no-treatment control condition. Again subjects' dietary intake was controlled by programme guidelines in all groups. Significant reductions in serum cholesterol were found in the intervention group only. A dose-dependent relationship between changes in behaviour and serum cholesterol was found by Gill *et al.* (1985), with only subjects who made the greatest changes in TAB having significant reductions in serum cholesterol.

Cooper (1982) examined the impact of brief meditation training on serum cholesterol levels of hypercholesterolaemic subjects. After exclusion of subjects who had radically modified their diet, changes following intervention in 12 subjects were compared with those of 11 control subjects. At one-year follow-up, a significant (12 per cent) reduction in serum cholesterol was found in the intervention group, with no such changes in the controls. In an uncontrolled study, Patel (1975) found serum cholesterol fell by a similar margin following eight weeks of training in relaxation skills. However, in a later controlled study (Patel *et al.*, 1985), no significant differences in changes in cholesterol emerged when compared with a minimal treatment control group.

Overall, the evidence is suggestive that stress management may in some cases significantly reduce serum cholesterol levels. However, well-controlled trials are still needed to determine the effectiveness of such interventions in the absence of other confounding factors such as exercise or dietary change, and for whom such interventions may be most effective. Dietary intervention may necessarily remain the primary intervention in hyperlipidaemia with other, adjunctive, interventions only used in dietary resistant cases, or where differing approaches may need to be combined in order to reduce levels of serum cholesterol to those considered safe.

HYPERTENSION

Whilst pharmacological treatment of hypertension has been successful in reducing morbidity to CHD even at mild hypertensive levels (diastolic blood pressure 90–104 mmHg), some failures to reduce morbidity have been reported and the absolute reduction in events has been small (e.g. Medical Research Council Working Party, 1985). Further, side-effects of medication are widely prevalent (Ramsay, 1985). Considerations such as these make the use of alternative, non-pharmacological, interventions particularly attractive.

The simplest of such interventions may be the daily self-monitoring of blood pressure, as this typically results in a gradual decline of measured blood pressure of between 7 and 11 mmHg (Chesney *et al.*, 1987; Glasgow *et al.*, 1982; Laughlin *et al.*, 1979) over periods of up to one year. This reduction may equal that resulting from interventions such as relaxation when measurements are taken in the clinic, but not for measurements taken in the home (Goldstein *et al.*, 1984) or the workplace (Chesney *et al.*, 1987). The cause of such a lowering effect is unclear. It may provide feedback to subjects' own attempts to reduce blood pressure. It may reflect a specific long-term habituation effect to measurement in the clinic. Thus, whilst self-monitoring of blood pressure may prove a useful first-line treatment of mild hypertension, changes in blood pressure need to be verified throughout the day if it is to be considered of therapeutic value.

Relaxation-based interventions provide the next simplest approach, particularly where this simply comprises the daily practice of relaxation or meditation. Early, uncontrolled, reports provided encouraging evidence of the effectiveness of such techniques, but these studies were beset by a number of methodological flaws including high drop-out rates (Benson *et al.*, 1976), the confounding of essential and secondary hypertensives in treatment (Datey *et al.*, 1976), changes of medication during treatment (Blackwell *et al.*, 1976), the use of placebo medication (Datey *et al.*, 1976), and the confounding of meditation with the self-monitoring of blood pressure (Blackwell *et al.*, 1976). Two controlled studies of the effect of meditation on blood pressure (Seer and Raeburn, 1980; Stone and DeLeo, 1976) reported a relatively greater reduction of blood pressure following subjects learning meditation techniques than in no-treatment conditions. Unfortunately, differential efficacy expectancies, which can powerfully affect blood pressure readings (Agras *et al.*, 1982), between treatment and no-treatment conditions weaken the strength of their findings.

Most interventions have attempted to integrate relaxation procedures into daily life. Patel and her colleagues (Patel *et al.*, 1981; Patel *et al.*, 1985) randomly allocated over 200 volunteers having two or more risk factors for CHD, including hypertension, to an intervention focusing on training in relaxation and meditation techniques or a minimal (information only) intervention. After eight weeks, blood pressures had fallen significantly more in intervention compared to control subjects, with a mean reduction of 20 mmHg *v.* 8 mmHg in SBP and 11 mmHg *v.* 4 mmHg in DBP of subjects initially within the hypertensive range. These differences were maintained or increased by three-month follow-up. By four-year follow-up (Patel *et al.*, 1985), although neither systolic nor diastolic pressures were as low as immediately post-treatment, those of the intervention subjects remained below initial levels and were significantly lower than control group levels. Similar relaxation procedures have also resulted in significantly greater reductions in blood pressure when compared with attention control procedures (Patel and Marmot, 1988; Patel and North, 1975) or no treatment (Jorgensen *et al.*, 1981; Southam *et al.*, 1982).

Comparisons of relaxation approaches with other more active interventions have generally favoured relaxation, although the more the alternative therapy provided means to effectively reduce stress, the less apparent the difference. Taylor *et al.* (1977) compared the effectiveness of medical treatment alone, or in conjunction with supportive psychotherapy, and relaxation training. Systolic blood pressure was reduced significantly more in the relaxation group than in the medical or psychotherapy conditions (13 mmHg *v.* 1 mmHg and 3 mmHg). Differences in DBP approached significance only (5 mmHg *v.* 0.3 mmHg and 2 mmHg). By six-month follow-up, although relaxation therapy still produced the greatest reduction in blood pressure, there were no statistically significant differences between any treatment group. However, low subject numbers and the inclusion of a number of normotensive subjects may have reduced the effect size. Using RET as a comparison treatment, Wadden (1984) failed to find any differences between relaxation training and cognitive therapy immediately post-intervention and at five-month follow-up, although the lack of placebo or control group leaves the effectiveness of either intervention open to question.

In an attempt to control for subjects' use of alternative blood pressure reduction strategies in the comparison group, Irvine *et al.* (1986) developed an ingenious placebo treatment consisting of mobility and flexibility exercises which subjects were told would lower peripheral resistance by the dilation of arterioles, and hence reduce blood pressure. Subjects were randomly allocated to this 'treatment' or relaxation training similar to that conducted by Patel. Expectancies of treatment outcome were equally high in each condition. Clinic measures of DBP in subjects not receiving concurrent medication were significantly lowered in the relaxation group (5 mmHg) but not exercise group (+4.5 mmHg) immediately following treatment and at three-month follow-up (3 mmHg *v.* 0 mmHg). Changes in SBP showed a similar trend, with substantial reductions in blood pressure in the treatment but not placebo condition immediately following intervention (6 mmHg *v.* +0.5 mmHg) and at follow-up assessment (7 mmHg *v.* +1 mmHg). Similar changes were found in medicated subjects. Whilst the results of this study suggest a specific long-term hypotensive effect of relaxation, it must be remembered that only subjects in the relaxation condition were advised that their hypertension might be related to stress, and their use of other methods (e.g. the avoidance of known stressors) to reduce their blood pressure cannot be excluded.

One key study (Agras *et al.*, 1983; Southam *et al.*, 1982) used semi-automatic blood pressure monitors to record subjects' blood pressure every 20 minutes throughout the day, to determine the degree of generalization of blood pressure reductions throughout the day following relaxation training. Subjects took part in an eight-week relaxation training programme followed by bimonthly booster sessions, or monitoring of blood pressure only. Immediately after treatment, differences strongly favouring the relaxation group were found for both systolic and diastolic blood pressure both in the clinic (–14/–13 mmHg *v.* –2/–2 mmHg) and worksite (–8/–6 mmHg *v.* +1/+2 mmHg). By one-year follow-up, the relaxation group continued to have significantly greater reductions in DBP when measured at the clinic (–13 mmHg *v.* –7 mmHg) and worksite (–7 mmHg *v.* + 1 mmHg), although a downward drift of SBP in the control group prevented the between-group differences achieving statistical significance.

The effectiveness of cognitive therapy in combination with relaxation has been carefully assessed in an impressive study by Chesney et al. (1987). They randomly allocated 158 unmedicated mildly hypertensive subjects into five treatment groups: relaxation training, relaxation training combined with cognitive restructuring, biofeedback-assisted relaxation, a combination of all three, and relaxation training combined with attempts to modify other hypertension-related variables (salt intake, caffeine, cigarettes, etc.). A control group had blood pressure readings taken at the same time as the treatment groups. Significant reductions in both SBP and DBP were found for all conditions on measures taken in the clinic, with no difference between groups on measures of BP taken at nine-weekly intervals over one year. However, both SBP and DBP showed significantly greater reductions favouring the intervention groups when measured at the worksite. Between-treatment comparisons revealed a significant additive effect of cognitive therapy to relaxation training on both clinic and worksite readings, approximating 5 mmHg, a statistically and clinically significant difference. No consistent differences were attributed to other intervention approaches.

In summary, a number of stress management strategies form a useful and applicable intervention in mild hypertension, as they can be effective in reducing blood pressure and, unlike medication, carry no risk of adverse side-effects. The optimal, or indeed minimally effective intervention is yet to be fully established. However, a two-stage intervention approach is suggested. In the first stage clients can be given information concerning blood pressure and its relationship to stress. Written information teaching relaxation skills, time management and so on could be given as well as details of other means of blood pressure reduction such as weight loss and salt restriction. This could be combined with self-monitoring of blood pressure during the working day as well as at home and in a clinic. Should this minimal intervention fail, a more complex stress management package may be implemented. The inclusion of some form of cognitive therapy appears an important outcome determinant, possibly because this can encourage and maintain appropriate behavioural change.

SUMMARY AND CONCLUSIONS

Stress management procedures have been shown to reduce the risk associated with three risk factors for CHD: TAB, hypertension and hypercholesterolaemia. That one form of intervention may effectively lower three independent risk factors for CHD is both encouraging and important. Risk factors combine multiplicatively, and small decreases on a number of risk factors may reduce the risk of CHD more than if only one risk factor is targeted (Johnston, 1989; Perkins, 1989), as in most medical interventions. Further, as stress-management-based interventions are not compromised by risk of reactions secondary to any treatment regime, one would expect them to reduce morbidity and mortality for CHD. The one study to report morbidity and mortality following preventive intervention (Patel et al., 1985) found that four years following intervention, significantly fewer mildly hypertensive men who had been taught stress management techniques had either died or developed symptoms of heart disease. More studies of this nature are needed.

Despite such optimism, it is important to note that stress management is far from the only psychological approach applicable to the modification of risk factors for CHD.

Self-management procedures may be more appropriate for interventions related to smoking and weight loss, whilst a variety of psychological methods may be applicable in maintaining adherence to exercise programmes shown effectively to reduce serum cholesterol levels and blood pressure (Blanchard *et al.*, 1988; Haskell, 1984).

As the evidence to sustain such interventions accrues, attention must be moved towards the development of systems of care into which such interventions can be integrated, and analysis of the cost-effectiveness of such interventions. Of particular pertinence to both these issues may be the development of community-wide interventions targeted at stress reduction. No major community-wide CHD prevention programme has yet focused on the teaching of stress management techniques using the mass media as a preventive strategy. Future programmes need to consider stress reduction strategies applicable to large populations, e.g., televised stress management courses, bibliotherapy, community education courses and so on. Such interventions, and indeed those previously discussed, need to be evaluated in terms of both absolute outcome and cost-effectiveness. Edgar and Schnieden (1989) provide a model of how such analysis could usefully be conducted in the case of treatment (in this case, pharmaceutical) for hypertension. More studies are required with long-term follow-up (both in terms of morbidity and subsequent usage of medication) before such issues can be thoroughly evaluated for stress management techniques.

At present, the primary care system appears central to many future service developments, as it is here that most risk factors will be identified, and many family doctors and their patients would welcome non-pharmacological intervention as an alternative to long-term medication (Bennett *et al.*, 1989). A Government White Paper (Department of Health and Social Security, 1987) has emphasized the role of the general practitioner and the primary care setting in preventive health. Psychologists have the skills, but need to make the opportunities, to become key practitioners within such a setting.

REFERENCES

Agras, W.S., Horne, M. and Taylor, C.B. (1982) Expectation and blood pressure-lowering effects of relaxation. *Psychosomatic Medicine*, **44**, 389–95.

Agras, W.S., Southam, M.A. and Taylor, C.B. (1983) Long-term persistence of relaxation-induced blood pressure lowering during the working day. *Journal of Consulting and Clinical Psychology*, **51**, 792–4.

Bennett, P., Blackall, M., Clapham, M., Little, S., Player, D. and Williams, K. (1989) The South Birmingham Coronary Prevention Project: A multidisiciplinary approach to the prevention of heart disease. *Community Medicine*, **11**, 90–6.

Bennett, P. and Carroll, D. (1989) The assessment of Type A behaviour: A critique. *Psychology and Health* **3**, 183–94.

Benson, H., Rosner, B.A., Marzetta, B.R. and Klemchuk, H.M. (1976) Decreased blood pressure in pharmacologically treated hypertensive patients who regularly elicited the relaxation response. *Lancet*, **i**, 289–91.

Blackwell, B., Bloomfield, S., Gartside, P., Robinson, A., Hanenson, I., Magenheim, H., Nidich, S. and Ziegler, R. (1976) Transcendental meditation in hypertension: Individual response patterns. *Lancet*, **i**, 223–6.

Blanchard, E.B., Martin, J.E. and Dubbert, P.M. (1988) *Non-drug Treatments for Essential Hypertension.* New York: Pergamon.

Blumenthal, J.A., Williams, R.B., Kong, Y.M., Schanberg, S.M. and Thompson, L.W. (1978) Type A behavior pattern and coronary atherosclerosis. *Circulation*, **58**, 634–9.

Bortner, R.W. (1969) A short rating scale as a potential measure of pattern A behavior. *Journal of Chronic Diseases*, **22**, 87–91.

Chesney, M.A., Black, G.W., Swan, G.E. and Ward, M.M. (1987) Relaxation training at the worksite. I. The untreated mild hypertensive. *Psychosomatic Medicine*, **49**, 250–73.

Cook, W.W. and Medley, D.M. (1954) Proposed hostility and pharisaic-virtue scales for the MMPI. *Journal of Applied Psychlogy*, **38**, 414–18.

Cooper, M.I. (1982) Effect of relaxation on blood pressure and serum cholesterol. *Activitas Nervosa Superior (Praha)*, Suppl. 3, 428–36.

Curtis, J. (1974) The effect of educational intervention on the Type A behavior pattern. Unpublished doctoral dissertation, University of Utah.

Datey, K.K., Deshmukh, S.N., Dalvi, C.P. and Vinekar, S.L. (1976) 'Shavasan': A yogic exercise in the management of hypertension. *Angiology*, **20**, 325–33.

Dembroski, T.M., MacDougall, J.M., Shields, J.L., Petitto, J. and Lushene, R. (1978) Components of the Type A coronary-prone behavior pattern and cardiovascular responses to psychomotor performance challenge. *Journal of Behavioural Medicine*, **1**, 159–76.

Department of Health and Social Security (1987) Promoting better health: The Government programme for improving primary health care. Command No. 249. London: HMSO.

Edgar, M.A. and Schnieden, H. (1989) The economics of mild hypertension programmes. *Social Science and Medicine*, **28**, 211–22.

Ellis, A. (1974) *Humanistic Psychotherapy: The Rational-emotive Approach.* New York: Julian Press and McGraw-Hill.

Francis, K.T. (1979) Psychologic correlates of serum indicators of stress in man: A longitudinal study. *Psychosomatic Medicine*, **41**, 617–28.

Friedman, M. and Powell, L.H. (1984) Diagnosis and quantitative assessment of Type A behavior: Introduction and description of the Videotaped Structured Interview. *Integrative Psychiatry*, **2**, 123–9.

Friedman, M. and Ulmer, D. (1984) *Treating Type A and Your Heart*. Englewood Cliffs, NJ: Erlbaum.

Friedman, M., Thoresen, C.E., Gill, J.J., Ulmer, D., Powell, L.H., Price, V.A., Brown, B., Thompson, L., Rabin, D., Breall, W.S., Bourg, E., Levy, R. and Dixon, T. (1986) Alteration of Type A behavior and its effect on cardiac recurrences in postmyocardial infarction patients: Summary of the Recurrent Coronary Prevention Project. *American Heart Journal*, **112**, 653–5.

Gallacher, J.E.J., Yarnell, J. and Buckland, D. (1988). Type A behaviour and prevalent heart disease in the Caerphilly study: Increase in risk or symptom reporting? *Journal of Epidemiology and Community Health*, **42**, 226–31.

Gill, J.J., Price, C.A., Friedman, M., Thoresen, C.E., Powell, L.H., Ulmer, D., Brown, B. and Drews, F.R. (1985) Reduction in Type A behavior in healthy middle-aged American military officers. *American Heart Journal*, **110**, 503–14.

Glasgow, M.S., Gaarder, K.R. and Engel, B.T. (1982) Behavioural treatment of high blood pressure. II. Acute and sustained effects of relaxation and systolic blood pressure biofeedback. *Psychosomatic Medicine*, **44**, 155–70.

Goldstein, I.B., Shapiro, D. and Thananopavaran, C. (1984) Home relaxation techniques for essential hypertension. *Psychosomatic Medicine*, **46**, 398–414.

Hart, K.E. (1984) Anxiety management training and anger control for Type A individuals. *Journal of Behavior Therapy and Experimental Psychiatry*, **15**, 133–9.

Haskell, W.L. (1984) Exercise-induced changes in plasma lipids and lipoproteins. *Preventive Medicine*, **13**, 23–36.

Haynes, S.G. and Mathews, K.A. (1988) The association of Type A behavior and cardiovascular disease – Update and critical review. In B.K. Houston and C.R. Snyder (eds), *Type A Behavior Pattern. Research, Theory and Intervention*. New York: Wiley.

Irvine, M.J., Johnston, D.W., Jenner, D.A. and Marie, G.V. (1986) Relaxation and stress management in the treatment of essential hypertension. *Journal of Psychosomatic Research*, **30**, 437–50.

Jenkins, C.D., Zyzanski, S.J. and Rosenman, R. (1979) *Jenkins Activity Survey*. New York: Psychological Corporation.

Jenni, M.A. and Wollersheim, J.P. (1979) Cognitive therapy, stress management training, and the Type A behavior pattern. *Cognitive Therapy and Research*, **3**, 61–73.

Johnston, D.W. (1989) Will stress management prevent coronary heart disease? *The Psychologist*, **2**, 275–8.

Jorgensen, R.S., Houston, B.K. and Zurowski, R.M. (1981) Anxiety management training in the treatment of essential hypertension. *Behavior Research and Therapy*, **19**, 467–74.

Laughlin, K.D., Fisher, L. and Sherrard, D.J. (1979) Blood pressure reductions during self-recording of home blood pressure. *American Heart Journal*, **98**, 629–34.

Levenkron, J.C., Cohen, J.C., Mueller, H.S. and Fisher, Jr, E.B. (1983) Modifying the Type A coronary-prone behavior pattern. *Journal of Consulting and Clinical Psychology*, **51**, 192–204.

Lovallo, W.R. and Pishkin, V. (1980) A psychophysiologocal comparison of Type A and B men exposed to failure and uncontrollable noise. *Psychophysiology*, **17**, 29–36.

McCranie, E.W., Simpson, M.E. and Stevens, J.S. (1981) Type A behavior, field dependence, and serum lipids. *Psychosomatic Medicine*, **43**, 107–116.

Medical Research Council Working Party (1985) MRC trial of treatment of mild hypertension: Principal results. *British Medical Journal*, **291**, 97–104.

Mitchell, J.R. (1984) What constitutes evidence on the dietary prevention of coronary heart disease? Cosy beliefs or harsh facts? *International Journal of Cardiology*, **5**, 287–98.

Novaco, R. (1978) Anger and coping with stress. Cognitive behavioral interventions. In J.P. Foreyt and D.P. Rathjen (eds), *Cognitive Behavior Therapy*. New York: Plenum.

Nunes, E.V., Frank, K.A. and Kornfeld, D.S. (1987) Psychologic treatment for the Type A behavior pattern and for coronary heart disease: A meta-analysis of the literature. *Psychosomatic Medicine*, **48**, 159–73.

Oldenburg, B., Perkins, R.J. and Andrews, G. (1985) Controlled trial of psychological intervention in myocardial infarction. *Journal of Consulting and Clinical Psychology*, **53**, 852–9.

Patel, C.H. (1975) Twelve-month follow-up of yoga and biofeedback in the management of hypertension. *Lancet*, **ii**, 62–4.

Patel, C. and Marmot, M. (1988) Can General Practitioners use training in relaxation and management of stress to reduce mild hypertension? *British Medical Journal*, **296**, 21–4.

Patel, C. and North, W.R. (1975). Randomized control trial of yoga and biofeedback in management of hypertension. *Lancet*, **2**, 62–4.

Patel, C., Marmot, M.G. and Terry, D.J. (1981) Controlled trial of biofeedback-aided behavioural methods in reducing mild hypertension. *British Medical Journal*, **282**, 2005–8.

Patel, C., Marmot, M.G., Terry, D.J., Carruthers, M., Hunt, B. and Patel, M. (1985). Trial of relaxation in reducing coronary risk: Four-year follow-up. *British Medical Journal*, **290**, 1103–6.

Perkins, D.A. (1989) Interactions among coronary heart disease risk factors. *Annals of Behavioural*

Medicine, 11, 3–11.

Price, V.A. (1988) Research and clinical issues in treating Type A behavior. In B.K. Houston and C.R. Snyder (eds), *Type A Behavior Pattern. Research, Theory and Intervention.* New York: Wiley.

Rahe, R.H., Tuffli, C.F., Suchor, R.J. and Arthur, R.J. (1973) Group therapy in the outpatient management of post-myocardial infarction patients. *Psychiatry in Medicine*, 4, 77–88.

Ramsay, L.E. (1985) Editorial Review. Mild hypertension: Treat patients, not populations. *Journal of Hypertension*, 3, 449–55.

Razin, A.M., Swencionis, C. and Zohman, L.E. (1986–7). Reduction of physiological, behavioral, and self-report responses in Type A behavior: A preliminary report. *International Journal of Psychiatry in Medicine*, 16, 31–47.

Review Panel on Coronary-Prone Behavior and Coronary Heart Disease (1981) Coronary-prone behavior and coronary heart disease: A critical review. *Circulation*, 63, 1199–1215.

Rosenman, R.H. (1978) The interview method of assessment of the coronary-prone behavior pattern. In T.M. Dembroski, S.G. Haynes and M. Feinleib (eds), *Coronary-prone behavior.* New York: Springer-Verlag.

Rosenman, R.H., Brand, R.J., Jenkins, C.D., Friedman, M., Straus, R. and Wurm, M. (1975) Coronary heart disease in the Western Collaborative Group Study: Final follow-up experience of 8½ years. *Journal of the American Medical Association*, 22, 872–7.

Roskies, E. (1987) *Stress management for the Healthy Type A. Theory and Practice.* New York: Guilford Press.

Roskies, E., Kearney, H., Spevack, M., Surkis, A., Cohen, C. and Gilman, S. (1979) Generalizability and duration of treatment effects in an intervention program for coronary-prone (Type A) managers. *Journal of Behavioral Medicine*, 2, 195–207.

Roskies, E., Seraganian, P., Oseasohn, R., Hanley, J.A., Collu, R., Martin, N. and Smilga, C. (1986) The Montreal Type A intervention project: Major findings. *Health Psychology*, 5, 45–69.

Roskies, E., Spevack, M., Surkis, A., Cohen, C. and Gilman, S. (1978) Changing the coronary-prone (Type A) behavior pattern in a nonclinical population. *Journal of Behavioral Medicine*, 1, 201–16.

Sanders, T.A.B. (1987) Diet and coronary heart disease. *Journal of the Royal Society of Health*, 5, 163–5.

Seer, P. and Raeburn, J.M. (1980) Meditation training and essential hypertension: A methodological study. *Journal of Behavioral Medicine*, 3, 59–71.

Southam, M.A., Agras, S., Taylor, B. and Kraemer, H.C. (1982) Relaxation training. Blood pressure lowering during the working day. *Archives of General Psychiatry*, 39, 715–17.

Spielberger, C.D., Jacobs, G.A., Russell, S. and Crane, R.S. (1983) Assessment of anger: The State–Trait Anger Scale. In J.N. Butcher and C.D. Spielberger (eds), *Advances in Personality Assessment*, Vol. 2. Hillsdale, NJ: Erlbaum.

Stone, R.A. and DeLeo, J. (1976) Psychotherapeutic control of hypertension. *New England Journal of Medicine*, **294**, 80–4.

Study Group of the European Atherosclerosis Society (1987) Strategies for the prevention of coronary heart disease: A policy statement of the European Atherosclerosis Society. *European Heart Journal*, **8**, 77–88.

Suinn, R. (1975) The cardiac stress management program for Type-A patients. *Cardiac Rehabilitation*, **5**, 13–15.

Suinn, R.M. and Bloom, L.J. (1978) Anxiety management training for pattern A behavior. *Journal of Behavioral Medicine*, **1**, 25–35.

Taylor, C., Farquhar, J.W., Nelson, E. and Agras, S. (1977) Relaxation therapy and high blood pressure. *Archives of General Psychiatry*, **34**, 339–42.

Thoresen, C.E., Friedman, M., Gill, J.K. and Ulmer, D.K. (1982) The Recurrent Coronary Prevention Project. Some preliminary findings. *Acta Medica Scandinavica*, (Suppl.) **660**, 172–92.

Thurman, C.W. (1983) Effects of a rational-emotive treatment program on Type A behavior among college students. *Journal of College Student Personnel*, **24**, 417–23.

Thurman, C.W. (1985a) Effectiveness of cognitive-behavioral treatments in reducing Type A behavior among university faculty. *Journal of Counselling Psychology*, **32**, 74–83.

Thurman, C.W. (1985b) Effectiveness of cognitive-behavioral treatments in reducing Type A behavior among university faculty – One year later. *Journal of Counselling Psychology*, **32**, 445–8.

Trevisan, M., Tsong, Y., Stamler, J., Tokich, T., Mojonnier, L., Hall, Y., Cooper, R. and Moss, D. (1983) Nervous tension and serum cholesterol: Findings from the Chicago coronary prevention evaluation program. *Journal of Human Stress*, March, 12–16.

Wadden, T.A. (1984) Relaxation therapy for essential hypertension: Specific or nonspecific effects. *Journal of Psychosomatic Research*, **28**, 53–61.

Wells, N. (1987) *Coronary Heart Disease: The Need for Action*. London: Office of Health Economics.

Williams, R.B. and Barefoot, J.C. (1988) Coronary-prone behavior: The emerging role of the hostility complex. In B.K. Houston and C.R. Snyder (eds), *Type A Behaviour Pattern. Research, Theory and Intervention*. New York: Wiley.

CHAPTER 9

Individual Strategies for Coping with Stress at Work: A Review

Philip Dewe, Tom Cox and Eamonn Ferguson

This chapter discusses some of the conceptual and methodological issues involved in the study of coping. It focuses on individual coping with work and work-related problems, and adopts a transactional framework for the definition of the key concepts of stress, appraisal and coping. It identifies and reviews 17 recent papers which are representative of the coping literature, as defined by the scope of the chapter. What it draws out of this review largely concerns issues of measurement, and four particular issues are flagged as important for future research. It concludes that there is a need for more and more adequate studies, particularly in relation to the classification and modelling of coping, and that the adequacy of those future studies should be partly judged in terms of how well they deal with the issues raised here.

INTRODUCTION

In setting their agenda for stress research in the 1980s, Payne *et al.* (1982) wrote that 'the coping component of the stress process is another "piece" of the puzzle worth examining'. Yet a decade later, despite the volume of research (Glowinkowski and Cooper, 1985), the intensity of the associated debates (Newton, 1989) and the widespread agreement on the importance of coping (Edwards, 1988), this part of the puzzle has not been satisfactorily resolved. The coping literature, as it stands, has been described as diverse (Endler and Parker, 1990), difficult to organize (Edwards, 1988) and fraught with problems (Cohen, 1987). However, these difficulties would not appear to be the result of any lack of advice as to the direction that coping research should take. Reviewers (Burke and Weir, 1980; Edwards, 1988; Newton, 1989, Schuler, 1984) have been remarkably consistent in identifying the issues that need to be addressed. These include agreeing on the relative meanings of *stress* and *coping*; and developing a research framework for the identification and measurement of coping strategies. This chapter provides a broad overview of progress made in these two areas, but also explores a number of methodological issues for future research.

THE CONCEPTS OF STRESS AND COPING

Two factors may contribute to the confusion surrounding the concept of *stress*. The first is the fact that stress continues to be defined in a number of different *ways* (Cox, 1978) and at a number of different *levels of analysis* (Cox et al., 1992). Thus stress has been treated as a stimulus, a response, or as a result of some interaction or imbalance between the individual and aspects of the environment (French *et al.*, 1974; McGrath, 1970; Cox 1978; 1985; 1990; Newton, 1989). The second and related issue is that concepts such as stress, demand and arousal (Cox, 1985) and stress and coping (Edwards and Cooper, 1988) have been frequently confounded. Some suggest that what is now needed when defining stress is a level of precision that avoids the temptation of all-inclusiveness (Eulberg *et al.*, 1988). Others argue that more focused research would place less reliance on the exact definition of the concept (Kasl, 1983). Still others argue that there are now more important controversies than how stress should be defined (Beehr and Franz, 1987).

The stress process

Many current theories of stress refer either implicitly or explicitly to the stress process, and in doing so seemingly place themselves in the framework of a general systems theory approach. If we are to advance our understanding of a stress process then, as Edwards and Cooper (1988) suggest, we must derive specific and conceptually distinct definitions and operations for the various elements which make up that process. Many theories also argue that stress is relational in nature (Lazarus and Launier, 1978; Cox, 1990) involving some sort of *transaction* between individuals and their environment. The concept of cognitive appraisal is central to this type of model (see Cox, 1990), and is often closely linked to that of coping.

Transactional definitions embrace three important themes (Burke and Weir, 1980; Schuler, 1984; Holroyd and Lazarus, 1982; Newton, 1989): (1) stress as a dynamic cognitive state, (2) representing a disruption in homeostatis or 'imbalance' and (3) giving rise to a requirement for resolution of that imbalance or restoration of homeostasis. Within the terms of such definitions, stress does not reside solely in aspects of the individual or of the environment, but in the perceived interplay between the two. As a result of an ongoing transaction with their environment, individuals are confronted with demands that impinge on their cognitive processes and which challenge their ability to cope or adapt (Pratt and Barling, 1988). Something must be at stake for a situation to give rise to stress (Cox, 1978; Folkman, 1982), and there must be an awareness that there is some deviation from normal functioning (Parker and De Cotiis, 1983). This is the key to the process of cognitive appraisal (Lazarus, 1966); the evaluation that individual well-being is threatened, challenged or harmed in some way (Holroyd and Lazarus, 1982). Such an appraisal is associated with a desire for resolution: it provides the motivation and direction for coping.

Stress relates to those *transactions* where environmental demands are perceived as challenging or taxing the individual's ability to cope, thus threatening well-being and necessitating individual effort to resolve the problem. However, while, at the conceptual level, researchers generally accept that stress should now be defined transactionally, empirically this perspective has still to be integrated into current measurement practice (Cox and Ferguson, 1991; Shirom, 1982).

Coping

The use of a transactional framework to define stress is usually associated with a conviction that coping is a major factor in the overall process (Folkman and Lazarus, 1980; Folkman *et al.*, 1986; Cox and Ferguson, 1991). As with stress, a number of different theoretical approaches have contributed to our understanding of this concept. These include coping as a psychoanalytical process; as a personal trait or style; as a description of situationally-specific strategies; as a sequence of stages; and as a classification or taxonomy of strategies (see for example Cox, 1987; Cox and Ferguson, 1991; Edwards, 1988; Folkman and Lazarus, 1980). From critiques of such approaches, three themes emerge. These are that coping should be viewed as: (1) *relational* in that it reflects the relationship between the individual and the environment (Folkman, 1982); (2) a process in contrast to the more traditional trait–content oriented approaches (Cox, 1987; Edwards 1988; Folkman *et al.*, 1986); and (3) integrative in nature linking the other components of the stress process (Cox and Ferguson, 1991; Schuler, 1984). Consistent with these themes, coping is defined here as: *the cognitions and behaviours, adopted by the individual following the recognition of a stressful encounter, that are in some way designed to deal with that encounter or its consequences.* Because the focus here is on work stress, coping in this chapter is defined in terms of the response to work or work-related encounters that tax individual abilities and resources. Although individuals are constantly in a state of adaptation, and while an understanding of how individuals deal with ordinary everyday events is important (Newton, 1989), the intent of the present definition is simply to reflect those encounters where normal functioning is significantly disrupted. One might also assume from this definition that coping is 'typically positioned' somewhere between stress and health in a simple linear model (Edwards and Cooper, 1988). This is not the intention, and the complexity of the overall stress process is emphasized and attention drawn to the involvement of both feedback and feedforward loops (Cox, 1978).

Cognitive appraisal and coping

The process through which individual and environmental factors combine to produce the cognitive state of stress, and thus influence coping, has received little attention in work settings (Edwards and Cooper, 1988). This process, cognitive appraisal (Lazarus, 1966), refers to those mechanisms that 'imbue a stressful encounter with meaning for the person' (Holroyd and Lazarus, 1982). Although tempting, it should not be assumed that such a process is rational (Edwards, 1988). However, within this context the notion of rationality does provide what Edwards (1988) terms a useful point of departure to describe the subsequent coping process. Two important interacting mechanisms are involved. The first – primary appraisal – refers to what is at stake (Folkman, 1982). It is the process by which individuals evaluate the significance of a particular encounter and its relevance for well-being (Folkman *et al.*, 1986). Essentially, primary appraisal asks the question, 'Is this encounter stressful?' (Cox, 1987). Secondary appraisal, on the other hand, refers to what can be done (Folkman, 1982). It is the evaluation of available coping resources and strategies. The convergence of the appraisal processes shapes the meaning of any encounter (Folkman, 1984), whether it is perceived as stressful, and how it can be dealt with. Coping is initiated in response to primary and secondary appraisal. These three processes are highly interdependent and influence each other during any encounter (Folkman, 1984). Identifying them as key elements of the stress process shifts the focus of research to understanding what individuals actually think and do in a stressful encounter (Holroyd and Lazarus, 1982), which tends to balance out the more traditional moderator paradigm. Often this paradigm has been over-used in work settings; the coping process has, on occasions, simply become the explanatory expedient of stressor–health relationships that cannot be easily understood (Dewe, 1989).

The need now is to develop measures which explicitly recognize the transactional nature of stress, and to develop methodologies where more enriched descriptions of the stress process are investigated through both quantitive and qualitative approaches (Bhagat and Beehr, 1985).

CURRENT RESEARCH INTO COPING: A REVIEW

A synthesis of reviewers' comments on coping research (for example, Aldwin and Revenson, 1987; Carver *et al.*, 1989; Endler and Parker, 1990; Amirkhan, 1990) indicates that three issues confront us. These are: (1) the appropriate concepts and methods for measuring coping, (2) the subsequent classification of coping strategies and (3) the utility of such findings. At times the question of settling an appropriate methodology tends to subsume the other issues. Essentially it reduces to a debate between theoretical and empirical approaches. To some (for example, Carver *et al.*, 1989), the difference between them is explained in terms of theory-based scale development and classification *v.* empirically based models where underlying dimensions emerge from statistical analysis. Part of the debate is between the generality imposed by theoretically derived classifications and the specificity that accompanies empirical solutions. Not surprisingly, it has been proposed that a more appropriate strategy might be to search for some middle ground which integrates the two approaches (Endler and Parker, 1990; Amirkhan, 1990).

A very common theoretical classification is that represented in the distinction between emotion-focused and problem-focused coping. The questions here are whether this classification is conceptually too broad, whether it can be sustained by the available data, and whether it offers any prediction of health-related outcomes. The evidence is that it is a weak distinction in the sense that it is not well supported as it stands, and it has only weak predictive power (Cox and Ferguson, 1991). However, despite this, it remains very popular in the literature, possibly because it is relatively unambiguous (Fleishman, 1984).

Whatever the actual architecture or classification of coping, it is clear that our ability to describe it will only improve as improvements are made in our ability to conceptualize coping, and in our methodology. Together these provide a framework for evaluating coping research in a work setting. However, because the literature on coping with work stress is so diverse and voluminous (Burke and Weir, 1980), criteria have to be established for any review of progress. Here, as elsewhere, these criteria involve: (1) limiting examination to the academic literature, (2) identifying articles on a co-citational basis and (3) selecting those that, broadly speaking, were measurement-oriented and directed towards identifying *individual* strategies used to cope with work stress. Areas such as social support, self-management (e.g., relaxation, meditation etc.) and organizational development are beyond the scope of this review. Seventeen studies were identified using these criteria (see Table 9.1), and are reviewed here as representative of the literature on coping as defined by the scope of this chapter. The review largely focuses on the methodologies used and related conceptual issues, although the question of utility is addressed.

Table 9.1 *Coping with work-related stress: individual coping strategies*

Empirical approaches	Theoretical approaches
Burke (1971)	Howard *et al.* (1975)
Hall (1972)	Kiev and Kohn (1979)
Burke and Belcourt (1974)	Feldman and Brett (1983)
Pearlin and Schooler (1978)	Stone and Neale (1984)
Menaghan and Merves (1984)	Latack (1986)
Parasuraman and Cleek (1984)	Dewe (1989)
Shinn *et al.* (1984)	Puffer and Brakefield (1989)
Newton and Keenan (1985)	Leana and Feldman (1990)
Dewe and Guest (1990)	

The most common approach to researching coping in a work setting appears to be taxonomic (Puffer and Brakefield, 1989; Cox, 1987) with researchers describing and categorizing coping behaviours that are broadly applicable to all work situations. The difficulties in further organizing this literature within a cohesive structure (Edwards, 1988) are discussed below.

Objectives and definitions

In terms of research *objectives*, only five of the studies selected (Burke, 1971; Dewe and Guest, 1990; Latack, 1986; Pearlin and Schooler, 1978; Stone and Neale, 1984) were primarily concerned with the development of coping measures. Measurement was, for the others, an issue, and at times was dealt with in some depth, but was not the main focus of the study. For those studies the main objectives were varied; e.g., concerned with investigating the effects of coping on strain and burnout (Shinn *et al.*, 1984), *or* understanding the relationship between coping and task complexity (Puffer and Brakefield, 1989), *or* identifying the coping strategies used by workers to deal with job loss (Leana and Feldman, 1990) *or* asking whether some coping strategies are more effective than others (Howard *et al.*, 1975).

In relation to the *definition* of coping, only six of the studies (Dewe and Guest, 1990; Parasuraman and Cleek, 1984; Pearlin and Schooler, 1978; Puffer and Brakefield, 1989; Shinn *et al.*, 1984; Stone and Neale, 1984) made any sort of structured offering. Furthermore, the most common practice was to draw on the definitions developed by Folkman (1984) or Lazarus and Folkman (1984). The remaining studies defaulted to letting the research 'speak for itself'. Here coping was implicitly defined either through the types of questions asked or the methodology used to classify strategies. In this way coping was: 'how individuals handled the event they described', *or* 'the sorts of things they did to cope with the stress and strain of their jobs', *or* 'those behaviours employees use when faced with stressful working conditions'. In such studies, what people do is frequently confused with how effective that behaviour is. The concept of coping can thus became value-laden (Cox and Ferguson, 1991).

Empirical and theoretically driven studies

It is possible to divide the studies under review into those that are empirical and those which are theory-driven.

EMPIRICAL STUDIES

Coping has been measured in a number of different ways, and there are no simple answers as to which approach is best (Cohen, 1987). However, there is a growing recognition that such measurement requires the development of techniques and methodologies that capture and describe what individuals *actually* think and do (Holroyd and Lazarus, 1982; Folkman, 1982; Schuler, 1985; Cox and Ferguson, 1991): although just asking people how they cope is not without its problems (Cohen, 1987; Edwards, 1988; Firth, 1985). The empirical approach typically works from open-ended questions; then uses content or factor analysis to derive a model which may then be applied back to understand the original questionnaire data. There are, of course, variations on this theme, and these have led to a wide range of coping strategies being identified in the work setting.

Researchers have expressed their initial enquiry – the open-ended question – in a variety of ways. Some have been focused in their approach, asking individuals to describe a particular incident and then report how they coped with it (Dewe and Guest, 1990; Menaghan and Merves, 1984; Newton and Keenan, 1985; Pearlin and Schooler, 1978; Ferguson, 1992). Others have asked individuals to focus on the emotional discomfort involved and described 'how they cope when their jobs occasionally demand a great deal of them' (Burke and Belcourt, 1974) *or* describe 'how they cope with the stress and strain of a particular job' (Shinn *et al.*, 1984). Other differences can also exist in the structuring of the initial enquiry. Researchers such as Newton and Keenan (1985) have argued that time limits should be imposed when using open-ended questions, to avoid problems such as memory errors. Other researchers, depending on their research objectives, have varied the instructions given, and asked individuals to describe strategies 'they found useful' or 'effective–ineffective' (Burke, 1971; Burke and Belcourt, 1974). At times, words such as *handle* or *deal* have been substituted for the term *cope*.

Content analysis and/or factor analysis have both been used to model coping strategies. When describing these models, researchers have either let the description emerge from the data (Dewe and Guest, 1990; Hall, 1972; Menaghan and Merves,

1984; Newton and Keenan, 1985; Pearlin and Schooler, 1978) *or* have classified the results on the basis of existing frameworks (Burke, 1971; Burke and Belcourt, 1974) *or* used very general descriptive categories such as adaptive–maladaptive (Shinn *et al.*, 1984). Again the problem-focused/emotion-focused classification is a popular device, and, at times, seems to be *forced* onto the available data regardless of other considerations. The researchers involved either suggest that their strategies can be broadly grouped according to these categories (Dewe and Guest, 1990) *or* describe those strategies in ways that reflect either a problem-focused ('direct action': Menaghan and Merves, 1984) or emotion-focused ('positive comparisons': Pearlin and Schooler, 1978) orientation.

THEORETICALLY DRIVEN STUDIES

Theoretical studies let existing theory guide the development of their models and scales; beginning with a set of hypothetical categories and testing this taxonomy in terms of its apparent applicability to particular stressful encounters (Amirkhan, 1990). The adequacy of this approach differs within these studies. Some researchers, for example, provide only minimal information on the literature reviewed, and on the derivation of their coping strategies (Kiev and Kohn, 1979; Leana and Feldman, 1990). Others simply state that their scale items were 'drawn from the research literature on stress and coping as well as the popular literature on time management' (Puffer and Brakefield, 1989). Still others use coping instruments developed by other authors (Dewe, 1989; Howard *et al.*, 1975). The more adequate studies offer a methodical and detailed analysis of the available literature and then a well-argued rationale for item selection and the subsequent developments (Feldman and Brett, 1983; Latack, 1986; Stone and Neale, 1984).

Other differences emerge between theoretically driven studies, when instructions for the completion of measures are considered. Some instructions are quite specific, asking individuals to respond with a particular situation in mind (Feldman and Brett, 1983; Leana and Feldman, 1990). Others are quite general and simply refer to coping with the pressure at work (Dewe, 1989) *or* the stress that originated in the job (Howard *et al.*, 1975). Latack (1986) uses both specific and general approaches, but in this case different coping categories are associated with different instructions. A different approach again is used by Stone and Neale (1984). Pointing to difficulties with internal consistency in traditional coping measures, they have developed an approach where, if a particular mode of coping is used, respondents were instructed to write in what they actually did.

Finally, when describing the different coping categories researchers have again relied on existing frameworks (Dewe, 1989; Howard *et al.*, 1975; Leana and Feldman, 1990) or let their theoretical review guide description (Latack, 1986; Feldman and Brett, 1983; Puffer and Brakefield, 1989; Stone and Neale, 1984).

Associated measurement issues

Not all researchers limited the scope of their investigations to the measurement of coping. Two other areas received attention: these were, not surprisingly, cognitive appraisal and coping outcomes. In relation to appraisal, the principal concern was *primary* appraisal and the meaning or significance that individuals give to events. A number of different research strategies were used. Two of the studies under review, Dewe (1989) and Newton and Keenan (1985), attempted to unpack the meaning of events through the use of open-ended questions. Individuals were asked to describe either 'why the incident was a problem to them' (Newton and Keenan, 1985), *or* 'say that the effect or impact was mainly positive or mainly negative' (Dewe, 1989). Both questions elicited data that were qualitatively distinct from descriptions of the events themselves. Other researchers approached the issue of appraisal from an attributional perspective asking, for example, for 'perceptual reactions to events' focusing on aspects of control and intensity (Leana and Feldman, 1990). Finally, Stone and Neale (1984) simply collected data against a range of descriptors (meaningless, desirable, acute–chronic, anticipated–unanticipated), all of which could be construed as relating to the meaning of events. The results from these different types of study are somewhat mixed, although sufficiently encouraging for appraisal to continue to be pursued as an area of study.

Finally, there is the question of whether coping helps? In general, the findings here on the effectiveness of coping are mixed, with researchers typically suggesting, for example, that at best the effects of coping may be neutral and, perhaps, at worst that to lower stress individuals should avoid maladaptive coping behaviours (Parasuraman and Cleek, 1984). The Pearlin and Schooler (1978) finding that individual coping appears to be least effective when dealing with the more impersonal problems of work received some support with reports that occupational problems may not be easily resolved by individual efforts alone (Menaghan and Merves, 1984), *and* that individual responses have little effect on problems (Shinn *et al.*, 1984) *and* that in situations such as job loss individuals may not be willing to use problem-focused coping strategies because they simply add to the stress (Leana and Feldman, 1990).

FUTURE DIRECTIONS

In general those engaged in coping research do not deny the difficulties surrounding the measurements of coping (Fleming *et al.*, 1984). Issues relating to the development of appropriate concepts and methodologies, and to the subsequent development and validity of models of coping, still require resolution (Cohen, 1987; Cox and Ferguson, 1991; Dewe and Guest, 1990). In the remaining section of this chapter the authors flag the future importance of some of the more methodological issues.

The first is the need to distinguish between coping *style* and coping *behaviour* in relation to the instructions used in measurement scales. Coping *styles* appear to be trait-like combinations of cognitions and behaviours expressed and/or described somewhat independently of the situation. Coping *behaviours*, by contrast, are what the person actually does in a particular situation. The former are context-free constructs, the latter are context-dependent. This distinction, as Newton (1989) suggests, is often reflected in the type of instructions that accompany coping measures. Asking individuals, for example, the general question of 'how they cope with the stress of work' may elicit responses that resemble a *style* of coping; whereas instructing individuals to focus on a particular event and then to describe how they coped with it is more likely to provide the actual *behaviours* used in a specific encounter. In some studies, what is intended as a measure of coping behaviour may in fact be a measure of coping style. At the same time, the instructions used with scales may also direct individuals to make another less obvious distinction – that between acute and ongoing coping. In this case, by giving more general instructions, individuals may be prompted to think in terms of ongoing stressors and stresses, thus identifying a different set of coping strategies from those elicited when directed to think in terms of a particular episode (Newton, 1989). Researchers should pay particular attention to the type of instructions given, and their impact on the coping strategies described.

The second issue relates to the use of composite – multi-item – scales to capture a particular type of coping. A low score, for example where a respondent checks only one or two items in a frequency scale, may not necessarily mean that the particular strategy is not frequently used; just that all items in the scale are not used as frequently as each other. While the difficulties in terms of internal reliability have been acknowledged (Stone and Neale, 1984), the difficulties in terms of interpretation have not.

Developing coping measures also requires a decision to be made as to the focus of the instrument or scale. This is the third issue – having to decide between occupationally specific or more general measures is not uncommon to work stress researchers. Occupationally specific measures have the advantage of capturing the unique subtitles of a particular work situation; however, they make cross-situational comparisons difficult (Folkman, 1982). More general measures support cross-sitation and cross-group comparisons, but can lose detail, where that is situation-specific, and may only weakly relate to the behaviour of any one occupational group. More generally developed measures may also fail to capture the influence of the particular organization's culture, thus somewhat limiting their explanatory potential.

The fourth issue here relates to the meaning individuals give to events and to the measurement of that meaning (Dewe, 1991). There are two interrelated points. The first point concerns those factors that make events stressful. The traditional response to stressor measurement seems to assume that the perceived presence of a potential stressor necessarily equates with an individual being under stress (Duckworth, 1985). Scales in use more commonly measure the extent to which demand is present than how that demand is evaluated (Newton, 1989). If, as Duckworth (1986) suggests, events should no longer be thought of as having some intrinsically negative power, then a distinction should be made between the events themselves and their meaning. The events, then, can be seen to represent a 'milieu' (Payne *et al.*, 1988). From this milieu meanings are derived, and the nature of experiences expressed. Whether that milieu is stressful or not will depend on how it is appraised. Individual evaluations of events may therefore be a more powerful predictor of affect than the events themselves (Dewe, 1989).

The second point here concerns whether traditional well-established measures of work stressors are prone to what Glowinkowski and Cooper (1985) describe as an 'inherent bias'. That is, as a result of economic and social changes since the event-based scales were developed, are some events now being overemphasized while other more significant ones are being ignored? In order for an event to be important, something has to be 'at stake' and there has to be a 'sensed judgement' (Holroyd and Lazarus, 1982) that something of value is about to be jeopardized. Without such judgements, and without measures which capture this facet of primary appraisal, research may unwittingly be asking individuals to respond to events which are neither important nore relevant.

Finally there is the question of how coping strategies should be classified. The difficulties involved have already been discussed; some of them relate to the attention and use that the emotion-focused/problem-focused distinction commands despite its apparent lack of predictive power. The available data support other, albeit related, interpretations. For example, the authors Cox and Ferguson (1991) have suggested that all coping serves one overall function: that of dealing with the emotional correlates of stressful events and creating a sense of control. Beyond this, they have argued, coping strategies have three functions rather than two. These are problem-solving, event reappraisal, and avoidance. Any one strategy, they have argued, may perform all or some of these three functions to some extent. All three functions serve to reduce the emotional consequences of problems but 'off-line' activities (avoidance) may be most directly targeted on managing emotion. It is argued here that such a scheme, or architecture, offers a more adequate classification both in terms of its fit to the available data and its likely predictive power. More and more adequate studies are required to unpack possible coping classifications and models, and explore their reliability and validity. The adequacy of these studies will be partly determined by the extent to which they recognize and deal with the issues discussed in this chapter.

This review has discussed conceptual and methodological issues associated with the study of coping. It has identified four issues which should be considered in future research. In doing so it has argued that stress and coping should be defined and measured within the framework of a transactional approach, and that the questions of how we classify and model coping remain open.

REFERENCES

Aldwin, C.M. and Revenson, T.A. (1987) Does coping help? A re-examination of the relation between coping and mental health. *Journal of Personality and Social Psychology*, **53**, 337–48.

Amirkhan, J.H. (1990) A factor analytically derived measure of coping. The coping strategy indicator. *Journal of Personality and Social Psychology*, **59**, 1066–74.

Beehr, T.A. and Franz, T.M. (1987) The current debate about the meaning of job stress. In J.M. Ivancevich and D.C. Ganster (eds), *Job Stress: From theory to suggestion*. New York: Haworth Press.

Bhagat, R.S. and Beehr, T.A. (1985) An evaluation summary and recommendations for future research. In T.A. Beehr and R.S. Bhagat (eds), *Human Stress and Cognition in Organizations: An integrated perspective*. New York: John Wiley.

Burke, R.J. (1971) Are you fed up with work? How can job tension be reduced? *Personnel*, **34**, 27–31.

Burke, R.J. and Belcourt, M.L. (1974) Managerial role stress and coping responses. *Journal of Business Administration*, **5**, 55–68.

Burke, R.J. and Wier, T. (1980) Coping with the stress of managerial occupations. In C.L. Cooper and R. Payne (eds), *Current Concerns in Occupational Stress*. Chichester: John Wiley.

Carver, C.S., Scheier, M.F. and Weintraub, J.K. (1989) Assessing coping strategies: A theoretically based approach. *Journal of Personality and Social Psychology*, **56**, 267–83.

Cohen, F. (1987) Measurement of coping. In S.V. Kasl and C.L. Cooper (eds), *Stress and Health: Issues in Research Methodology*. Chichester: John Wiley.

Cox, T. (1978) *Stress*. London: Macmillan.

Cox, T. (1985) The nature and measurement of stress. *Ergonomics*, **28**, 1155–63.

Cox, T. (1987) Stress, coping and problem solving. *Work and Stress*, **1**, 5–14.

Cox, T. (1990) The recognition and measurement of stress: Conceptual and methodological issues. In N. Corlett and J. Wilson (eds), *Evaluation of Human Work*. London: Taylor & Francis.

Cox, T. and Ferguson, E. (1991) Individual differences, stress and coping. In C.L. Cooper and R. Payne (eds), *Personality and Stress: Individual differences in the stress process*. Chichester: John Wiley.

Cox, T., Kuk, G. and Leiter, G. (1992) Burnout, health, work stress and organizational health. In W. Schaufeli and C. Maslach (eds), *Professional Burnout: Recent Developments in Theory and Research* New York: Hemisphere.

Dewe, P.J. (1989) Examining the nature of work stress: Individual evaluations of stressful experiences and coping. *Human Relations*, **42**, 993–1013.

Dewe, P.J. (1991) Primary appraisal, secondary appraisal and coping: Their role in stressful work encounters. *Journal of Occupational Psychology*, **64**, 331–51.

Dewe, P.J. and Guest, D.E. (1990) Methods of coping with stress at work: A conceptual analysis and empirical study of measurement issues. *Journal of Organisational Behaviour*, **11**, 135–50.

Duckworth, D. (1985) Is the 'organisational stress' construct a red herring? A reply to Glowinkowski and Cooper. *Bulletin of the British Psychological Society*, **35**, 401.

Duckworth, D. (1986) Managing without stress. *Personnel Management*, 40–3.

Edwards, J.R. (1988) The determinants and consequences of coping with stress. In C.L. Cooper and R. Payne (eds), *Causes, Coping and Consequences of Stress at Work*. Chichester: John Wiley.

Edwards, J.R. and Cooper, C.L. (1988) Research in stress, coping and health: Theoretical and methodological issues. *Psychological Medicine*, **18**, 15–20.

Endler, N.S. and Parker, J.D.A. (1990) Multidimensional assessment of coping: A critical evaluation. *Journal of Personality and Social Psychology*, **58**, 844–54.

Eulberg, J.R., Weekley, J.A. and Bhagat, R.S. (1988) Models of stress in organisational research: A metatheoretical perspective. *Human Relations*, **41**, 331–50.

Feldman, D.C. and Brett, J.M. (1983) Coping with new jobs: A comparative study of new hires and job changers. *Academy of Management Journal*, **26**, 258–72.

Ferguson, E. (1992) Stress, personality and health. Unpublished Ph.D. thesis, University of Nottingham.

Firth, J. (1985) Personnel meanings of occupational stress: Cases from the clinic. *Journal of Occupational Psychology*, **58**, 139–48.

Fleishman, J.A. (1984) Personality characteristics and coping patterns. *Journal of Health and Social Behaviour*, **25**, 229–44.

Fleming, R., Baum, A. and Singer, J.E. (1984) Towards an integrative approach to the study of stress. *Journal of Personality and Social Psychology*, **46**, 939–49.

Folkman, S. (1982) An approach to the measurement of coping. *Journal of Occupational Behaviour*, **3**, 95–107.

Folkman, S. (1984) Personnel control and stress and coping processes: A theoretical analysis. *Journal of Personality and Social Psychology*, **46**, 839–52.

Folkman, S. and Lazarus, R.S. (1980) An analysis of coping in a middle aged community sample. *Journal of Health and Social Behaviour*, **21**, 219–39.

Folkman, S., Lazarus, R.S., Dunkel-Schetter, C., de Longis, and Gruen, R.J. (1986) Dynamics of a stressful encounter: Cognitive appraisal, coping and encounter outcomes. *Journal of Personality and Social Psychology*, **50**, 992–1003.

French, J.P.R., Rodgers, W. and Cobb, S. (1974) Adjustment as person–environment fit. In G.V. Coelho, D.A. Hamburg and J.E. Adams (eds), *Coping and Adaptation*. New York: Basic Books.

Glowinkowski, S.P. and Cooper, C.L. (1985) Current issues in organisational stress research. *Bulletin of the British Psychological Society*, **38**, 212–16.

Hall, D.T. (1972) A model of coping with role conflict: The role behaviour of college educated woman. *Administrative Science Quarterly*, **17**, 471–86.

Holroyd, K.A. and Lazarus, R.S. (1982) Stress, coping and somatic adoption. In L. Goldberger and S. Breznitz (eds), *Handbook of Stress: Theoretical and Clinical Aspects*. New York: Free Press.

Howard, J.H., Rechnitzer, P.A. and Cunningham, D.A. (1975) Coping with job tension – effective and ineffective methods. *Public Personnel Management*, **4**, 317–26.

Kasl, S.V. (1983) Perusing the link between stressful life experiences and disease: A time for reappraisal. In C.L. Cooper (ed.), *Stress Research: Issues for the eighties*. Chichester: John Wiley.

Kiev, A. and Kohn, V. (1979) *Executive Stress*. New York: AMACOM.

Latack, J.C. (1986) Coping with job stress: Measures and future directions for scale development. *Journal of Applied Psychology*, **71**, 377–85.

Lazarus, R.S. (1966) *Psychological Stress and the Coping Process*. New York: McGraw-Hill.

Lazarus, R.S. and Folkman, S. (1984) *Stress Appraisal and Coping*. New York: Springer.

Lazarus, R.S. and Launier, R. (1978) Stress related transactions between person and environment. In L.A. Pervin and M. Lewis (eds), *Perspectives in International Psychology*. New York: Plenum.

Leana, C.R. and Feldman, D.C. (1990) Individual responses to job loss: Empirical findings from two field studies. *Human Relations*, **11**, 1155–81.

McGrath, J.E. (ed.) (1970) *Social and Psychological Factors in Stress*. New York: Holt, Rinehart & Winston.

Menaghan, E.G. and Merves, E.S. (1984) Coping with occupational problems: The limits of individual efforts. *Journal of Health and Social Behaviour*, **25**, 406–23.

Newton, T.J. (1989) Occupational stress and coping with stress: A critique. *Human Relations*, **42**, 441–61.

Newton, T.J. and Keenan, A. (1985) Coping with work-related stress. *Human Relations*, **38**, 107–26.

Parasuraman, S. and Cleek, M.A. (1984) Coping behaviour and managers' affective reactions to role stressors. *Journal of Vocational Behaviour*, **24**, 179–83.

Parker, D.F. and De Cotiis, T.A. (1983) Organisational determinants of job stress. *Organisational Behaviour and Human Performance*, **32**, 160–77.

Payne, R.A., Jick, T.D. and Burke, R.J. (1982) Whither stress research? An agenda for the 1980s. *Journal of Occupational Behaviour*, **3**, 131–45.

Pearlin, L.I. and Schooler, C. (1978) The structure of coping. *Journal of Health and Social Behaviour*, **19**, 2–21.

Pratt, L.I. and Barling, J. (1988) Differing between daily events, acute and chronic stressors: A framework and its implications. In J.J. Hurrell, L.R. Murphy, S.L. Sauter and C.L. Cooper (eds), *Occupational Stress: Issues and Developments in Research*. London: Taylor & Francis.

Puffer, S.M. and Brakefield, J.T. (1989) The role of task complexity as a moderator of the stress and coping process. *Human Relations*, **3**, 199–217.

Schuler, R.S. (1984) Organisational stress and coping: A model and overview. In A.S. Sethi and R.S. Schuler (eds), *Handbook of Organisational Stress Coping Strategies.* Cambridge, MA: Ballinger.

Schuler, R.S. (1985) Integrative transactional process model of coping with stress in organisations. In T.A. Beehr and R.S. Bhagat (eds), *Human Stress and Cognition in Organisations: An Integrative Perspective.* New York: John Wiley.

Shinn, M., Rosario, M., Morch, H. and Chestnut, D.E. (1984) Coping with job stress and burnout in the human services. *Journal of Personality and Social Psychology*, **46**, 864–76.

Shirom, A. (1982) What is organisational stress? A facet analytic conceptualization. *Journal of Occupational Behaviour*, **3**, 21–38.

Stone, J.A. and Neale, J.M. (1984) New measure of daily coping: Development and preliminary results. *Journal of Personality and Social Psychology*, **46**, 892–906.

CHAPTER 10

Coping with Work-related Stress: A Critique of Existing Measures and a Proposal for an Alternative Methodology

Michael P. O'Driscoll and Cary L. Cooper

Numerous instruments have been developed to assess coping strategies used by individuals during stressful transactions. We discuss some of the problems and limitations inherent in existing coping measures, along with issues surrounding their development. An alternative approach to examining coping with stress is proposed, based upon critical incident analysis of stressors experienced by individuals, the behaviours they exhibit and the outcomes of those behaviours. While some studies have used aspects of this technique, the present proposal offers a framework for assessing the interrelationships between stressors, behaviours and consequences.

INTRODUCTION

As part of a general concern about the impact of work conditions on the health and well-being of employees, considerable energy has been devoted in recent years to increasing our knowledge about stress experienced at work (Cooper and Payne, 1988; Quick *et al.*, 1992). Thirty years of systematic study have generated a substantial body of evidence on factors which contribute to stress – the 'sources' of stress (Cooper, 1996). Much less is known, however, about how individuals deal with or manage the stress they experience, and about effective methods of coping with work-related stress. Despite numerous efforts to examine coping strategies, our understanding of the stress–coping process remains incomplete (Edwards, 1988).

The importance of understanding coping mechanisms has been underlined by several investigators (e.g., Aldwin and Revenson, 1987; Cox and Ferguson, 1991; Lazarus and Folkman, 1984), who suggest that coping behaviours can minimize the impact of stress and alleviate its negative consequences. By contrast, lack of effective stress management may lead to significant decrements in well-being, dissatisfaction, feelings of disengagement from the job, and reduced job performance. Prolonged maladaptive coping may ultimately induce a chronic, highly debilitating form of stress known as *burnout* (Leiter, 1991). There is general agreement that coping forms part of the person–environment transaction which occurs when an individual perceives a situation as stressful (Latack and Havlovic, 1992). Recently, Dewe and his colleagues (see Chapter 9) have described coping as 'cognitions and behaviours adopted by the individual following the recognition of a stressful encounter, that are in some way designed to deal with that encounter or its consequences' (Dewe *et al.*, 1993, p. 7). This simple definition highlights the major elements of the coping process: occurrence of an event which impinges upon the person, appraisal of that event as threatening to oneself, and manifestation of some cognitive or behavioural response to alleviate or remove the threat.

Nevertheless, although stress researchers view coping as a major component of the overall stress process (Dewe *et al.*, 1993; Folkman *et al.*, 1986), there has been disagreement over the functions and consequences of coping. For example, Cox and Ferguson (1991) have noted that confusion over whether coping should be treated as a mediating link between stressors and psychological strain or as a moderator of the stress–strain relationship (the 'stress-buffering hypothesis') has clouded the debate over the potential functions of coping behaviours.

In addition to conceptual difficulties, a major reason for lack of progress in increasing our knowledge of coping processes centres around the problem of measurement. How people cope with stress has been assessed via a multitude of diverse methods (Cohen, 1987; Dewe *et al.*, 1993; Latack and Havlovic, 1992), so it is hardly surprising that there is inconsistency in the findings which have emerged from research. The purpose of the present chapter is (1) to examine some of the limitations inherent in extant approaches to the development of stress–coping measures and (2) to suggest an alternative methodology, based on critical incident analysis of both the stressors which individuals encounter and the coping behaviours which they utilize in their efforts to manage their environments.

This approach is modelled on behavioural description interviewing in personnel selection, in which the antecedents, behaviours and consequences of behaviour are elicited via direct questioning of individuals about their experiences. Although a few studies (e.g. Newton and Keenan, 1985) have used critical incident analysis to explore some aspects of the stress-coping process, the research strategy proposed here integrates all three components of the stress process: stressors, coping behaviours and coping outcomes.

CONCEPTS AND METHODS OF COPING ASSESSMENT

Several reviews of stress-coping instruments have been published recently (Cohen, 1987; Dewe *et al.*, 1993; Latack and Havlovic, 1992). Our intention is not to describe in detail the various methods which have been utilized to assess coping strategies. Nevertheless, it is important to highlight some of the problems and limitations inherent in extant approaches.

Before discussing these, there are five major issues surrounding the development of coping measures which are especially pertinent in this context:

1. the distinction between coping styles and behaviours,
2. the specificity of coping responses,
3. deductive *v.* inductive approaches to assessing coping,

4. general stress *v.* specific stressors (the focus of coping),
5. predetermined *v.* elicited stressors.

Coping styles v. coping behaviours

Coping 'styles' refer to consistent and stable preferences for particular strategies for dealing with stressful situations; typically they are elicited by asking individuals how they usually cope with stress (Pearlin and Schooler, 1978). In contrast, 'coping behaviours' (or processes) refer to the responses which individuals actually make (or say they make) in stressful transactions (Folkman and Lazarus, 1986).

Folkman and Lazarus (1980; 1986) have argued that coping styles are too broad to be useful and are unrelated to the context in which coping occurs. In addition, research has found little correspondence between preferred styles and actual coping responses (Carver *et al.*, 1989; Cohen, 1987; Edwards, 1988). Furthermore, the capacity of coping styles to predict outcomes (such as enhanced well-being) has not been well demonstrated, nor have these styles been found to moderate (buffer) the impact of stressors on levels of experienced strain (Edwards, 1988). In sum, while there may sometimes be reasons for exploring global preferences (Newton, 1989), understanding the coping process requires probing concrete behavioural dimensions.

Studies focusing on coping *responses* have illustrated that coping behaviours can be differentiated and may be predictive of personal outcomes for individuals. Again, however, the findings have not been totally consistent across studies, nor have coping behaviours always been shown to moderate the stressor–stain relationship (Aldwin and Revenson, 1987; Billings and Moos, 1984; Parasuraman and Cleek, 1984).

Specificity of coping

Some approaches to coping, such as Lazarus and Folkman's Ways of Coping questionnaire and the Health and Daily Living Form (Billings and Moos, 1981; 1984), focus on broad categories of coping behaviour. Dewe and Guest (1990), among others, have queried whether these categories adequately capture the range of potential coping responses. A somewhat different criticism has been voiced by Newton and Keenan (1985), who questioned whether universal coping strategies actually exist, or whether individuals adopt specific strategies in different stressful situations. A start was made in this direction by Firth-Cozens and Morrison (1986; 1989) among fourth-year medical students and junior doctors, and by West and Savage (1988a, b) among health visitors. Firth-Cozens and Morrison (1989) explored stress and coping in a group of 173 pre-registration doctors. They asked these medical students and first-year residents to describe a recent stressful event and the specific way in which they coped with it. They found that dealing with death, senior doctors, personal mistakes and overload were the main stressors, with the most frequently used coping strategies being 'problem-solving' and 'asking for help'. West and Savage (1988a) examined the coping mechanism used by 60 health visitors, who were asked to record each stressful event over a 15-day period and how they coped with each (selected from a predetermined list of coping strategies, e.g.

'thinking about the solutions of the problem', 'accepting the problem', 'diverting attention from the problem'). They were able to match a specific stressor with a particular coping response. Both of these studies are important first steps in highlighting the specificity of coping. Further exploration, however, is needed to further refine the way in which specific stressor dimensions elicit different coping behaviours.

Deductive v. inductive generation of measures

Some instruments for assessing coping strategies (such as Lazarus and Folkman's problem-focused and emotion-focused indices) were constructed deductively, from existing research and literature. Indices of coping with job stress have been derived in this manner by Stone and Neale (1984) and Latack (1986). In contrast, the inductive approach elicits from individuals the specific responses they exhibited in particular stressful transactions then combines those responses into meaningful categories. This methodology has been advocated recently by Cox and Ferguson (1991) and is illustrated in research conducted by Newton and Keenan (1985). The major advantage of the inductive over the deductive approach is that the former makes no assumptions about how individuals might respond in specific situations and is therefore more likely to have ecological validity. It therefore avoids placing any restriction on the types of behaviours which individuals may report exhibiting during stressful transactions.

Focus of coping

Investigations also differ in terms of the focus of coping. While some have examined coping with stress in general, others refer to specific stressors. These divergent foci may make a substantial difference to the coping responses reported by individuals (Stone *et al.*, 1991). Pearlin and Schooler (1978), for instance, asked their respondents how they 'usually coped' with stress, whereas Folkman and Lazarus (1986; Folkman *et al.*, 1986) examined responses to particular events. Studies investigating global coping have been criticized as lacking a target for the coping response (Edwards, 1988; Kinicki and Latack, 1990; Newton, 1989).

Predetermined v. elicited stressors

The majority of job-related stress studies have solicited respondents' perceptions of the impact of a predetermined set of potential stressors, such as role demands, human resource management practices, or job/off-job conflict. While these studies provide valuable information about reactions to specified work-related events, they cannot identify which of all the potential sources of stress are most salient to individuals. Alternatively, several studies (e.g. Carver *et al.*, 1989; Dewe and Guest, 1990; Holahan and Moos, 1990; Newton and Keenan, 1985; Schwartz and Stone, 1993) have asked respondents themselves to identify stressful experiences which they have confronted, although few have focused specifically on workplace stressors (Dewe, 1991; Newton and Keenan, 1985). Compared with *a priori* selection of stressors, this approach enables respondents to report events or encounters which are important to themselves, again enhancing ecological validity (Newton, 1989). A potential disadvantage is that a vast array of idiosyncratic stressors might be generated, making it difficult to draw generalizable conclusions. Latack (1986) observed, however, that individuals tended to use similar coping strategies across a range of different role stressors, so perhaps this problem is not as serious as it appears.

The issues discussed above create dilemmas for researchers attempting to explore coping with stress, making it difficult to draw conclusions about the use and effectiveness of various coping strategies. In addition to these general issues, methodological difficulties associated with the assessment of coping have limited the development of knowledge about stress-coping processes. In the following section, we outline some of the more pervasive and troublesome of these problems.

METHODOLOGICAL PROBLEMS WITH EXTANT COPING MEASURES

Recent reviews (Cohen, 1987; Edwards, 1988; Latack and Havlovic, 1992) have pointed to several limitations of coping measures, along with the failure to consistently demonstrate the utility of these measures. Some of the more critical difficulties with existing methods for assessing coping are summarized below.

INTERNAL RELIABILITY

Substantial variations in the internal reliabilities of coping scales have been documented. In their review of the empirical literature, Latack and Havlovic (1992) found an average alpha coefficient of 0.71 across 15 studies which reported this statistic, varying from 0.38 to 0.92. For example, the most frequently utilized coping instrument, Lazarus and Folkman's Ways of Coping questionnaire, has demonstrated considerable variance in its internal reliability estimates, which have ranged from 0.35 to 0.85 (Edwards and Baglioni, 1993; Folkman and Lazarus, 1986; McCrae, 1984). Billings and Moos' Health and Daily Living Form has displayed similar vagaries in its reliability. Billings and Moos (1984) obtained alpha coefficients as low as 0.41 to 0.66, while Holahan and Moos (1990) reported alphas of 0.83 for approach coping, but only 0.60 for avoidance coping.

Latack (1986) has constructed one of the few instruments which specifically examines coping with stress in work contexts. Internal reliability coefficients for her subscales were generally higher than those reported for either the Ways of Coping or the Health and Daily Living Form, ranging from 0.54 to 0.85, but again some of the alphas were marginal. Dewe and his colleagues (Dewe, 1991; Dewe and Guest, 1990) have also developed a job-related stress coping instrument which, with the possible exception of two subscales, has shown reasonable reliability (0.66 to 0.81; Dewe, 1991).

Coping measures derived to focus on specific forms of stress have fared no better than general coping instruments. For example, in Schonfeld's (1990) assessment of five types of coping strategy used by teachers, alpha coefficients range from 0.61 to 0.76, while Stone and Neale's (1984) study of ten coping modes obtained an average reliability estimate of just 0.61. Finally, Kinicki and Latack's (1990) measure of coping with involuntary job loss displayed alphas ranging from 0.44 to 0.73; three factors showed unacceptable reliability, and the remaining three were marginal at best.

This brief overview of internal reliability highlights a major area of difficulty for many existing coping measures. Research has obtained coefficients which are generally lower than desirable for establishing the adequacy of coping scales, suggesting one possible reason for their haphazard performance in job stress research. In addition, low internal consistency also raises serious questions about the validity of these instruments.

CONSTRUCT VALIDATION

Unfortunately there have been few attempts to confirm the factor structures of coping measures and varying factor structures for the same instruments have been obtained (Edwards, 1988). For example, efforts to replicate the original factor structure of the Ways of Coping checklist have resulted not only in differing numbers of factors, but also different assignments of coping behaviours to factors (Aldwin and Revenson, 1987; Cohen, 1987; Latack and Havlovic, 1992).

A further validity issue is that coping dimensions, particularly those which are theoretically-derived, may not cover the full range of important coping behaviours. Amirkhan (1990) has observed that, while deductive taxonomies are often generalizable and have categories which are sufficiently broad to describe coping processes across individuals and contexts, they nevertheless fail to include some important strategies. Research exploring the use of predetermined coping strategies may not detect whether the most salient behaviours have been assessed.

CONVERGENT AND DISCRIMINANT VALIDITY

There are indications of considerable overlap between some modes of coping which should be empirically distinct, as well as a lack of relationship between similarly-named coping dimensions. The functions served by different coping mechanisms may overlap in some contexts, hence producing a significant correlation between strategies (Amirkhan, 1990). Equally problematical, however, is that similar dimensions from different instruments sometimes bear little relationship to each other (Cohen, 1987), suggesting either that they tap into separate domains of coping or that substantial measurement unreliability exists in these instruments. Either way, evidence concerning interrelationships between coping scales is disturbing.

PREDICTIVE VALIDITY

A final problem with existing coping measures is that frequently they fail to predict important individual outcomes. For example, Folkman *et al.* (1986) found that only two out of eight Ways of Coping subscales discriminated significantly between satisfactory and unsatisfactory outcomes for individuals, and Cox and Ferguson (1991) concluded that Lazarus and Folkman's typology has to date demonstrated weak predictive power.

Although some studies have obtained direct relationships between coping and well-being (Edwards, 1988), the stress-buffering influence of coping strategies has not been demonstrated consistently. Cohen (1987) and Nelson and Sutton (1990), for instance, have observed that there is no evidence that Billings and Moos' (1981) coping dimensions have stress-attentuation (buffering) effects, while Aldwin and Revenson (1987) noted no clear consensus on which modes of coping are most effective. In all, there would appear to be no compelling evidence that current methods of assessing coping tap into behaviours which have a substantial impact on stress-related experiences.

AN ALTERNATIVE APPROACH TO THE ASSESSMENT OF COPING

As indicated above, one of the major reasons for difficulties associated with existing approaches to the measurement of coping is the very manner in which these instruments have been constructed. In particular, while some investigators have elicited specific stressors from individuals (e.g. Amirkhan, 1990; Carver *et al.*, 1989; Holahan and Moos, 1990; Schwartz and Stone, 1993) and others have examined their actual coping behaviours (e.g. Dewe and Guest, 1990), with one exception (Newton and Keenan, 1985) research on stress-coping behaviours has not simultaneously explored both specific stressors and actual responses to those stressors.

There has, therefore, been little effort to link the specific coping responses which individuals exhibit to the actual source of stress. We propose that this is essential to gain a complete understanding of the process of coping. In the remainder of this chapter we outline an approach which enables a mapping of coping behaviours on to the sources of stress which are experienced by individuals in work contexts. This approach builds upon suggestions raised by Cox and Ferguson (1991) and extends Newton and Keenan's research by also focusing on the outcomes of coping efforts.

Critical incident analysis (CIA), first described in detail by Flanagan (1954), forms the basis of the method advocated here. Applied to the stress-coping process in work settings, CIA entails asking individuals to describe stressful transactions in terms of three elements: (1) the antecedents or circumstances in which the stress occurred, (2) their responses in that situation, along with the responses of other people, and (3) the consequences of both their own and other individuals' behaviour.

Description of the stressful transaction

The first step in critical incident analysis is to interview individuals to obtain a detailed description of job-related events which they have experienced recently (e.g. in the past few months) which they believe to have placed demands upon them or caused them problems or difficulties. Characteristics of the transactions which have impinged upon the person are elicited in these descriptions. It is important to ensure that these antecedents are described specifically (e.g. 'had an argument with my boss about *the time it took me to complete* a report'), rather than in vague or general terms (e.g. 'had an argument with my boss about a report'). The first illustration specifies the exact nature of the argument, whereas the second provides insufficient detail on what the 'problem' actually was. To increase the representativeness of stressors elicited via this procedure, it is desirable to obtain two or three stressful incidents from each individual.

As with behavioural description interviewing, which the CIA approach to stress-coping measurement is modelled upon, as far as possible emotive terminology should be avoided. Rather than describing events as 'stressful', a term which is laden with subjective interpretation, it is preferable to ask individuals to think of situations which have had a disruptive effect on their work or created undue pressures for them. In addition to the problem of idiosyncratic definition, use of the term 'stress' may predispose individuals to relate only those situations in which they have not coped, hence limiting the opportunity to explore effective coping behaviours. Ideally, CIA should elicit a range of both effective and less effective coping responses.

Another dimension of stressful transactions is their duration. Some incidents, such as the illustration given above, may be short term, infrequently occurring events, whereas others (e.g. workload problems) may be continuous and persist for a longer period. Clearly, different forms of coping may be displayed in respect of these types of stressor, hence it is important to record the duration and frequency of the transaction described.

Responses to the stressors

The second stage of the critical incident procedure is to ask individuals to describe specific behaviours which they exhibited when confronted by each particular stressor. Using the above example, an individual might indicate that he 'went away and waited till my boss calmed down, then talked with her about this issue'. This represents an illustration of specific behaviours which the person has displayed in response to the stressor. The fact that it contains two separate behaviours ('went away' and 'talked with her') is perfectly acceptable within the framework of critical incident analysis – it would simply be recorded that this person showed two responses in this encounter.

The key to this phase is to ensure that behaviours displayed by the person him/herself are elicited. Again using the above illustration, if the individual said 'my boss walked off before the matter was resolved', this would be insufficient in terms of describing what the focal person had done in that situation. A description of that person's behaviour is essential, even if no overt response was made (e.g. 'I didn't do anything'). In this case, follow-up questions should probe whether the person made any 'internal' (cognitive or emotional) response, even if no action was taken.

It is important to avoid implicit or explicit reference to coping or coping effectiveness when questioning individuals about their behaviour (Cohen, 1987; Cox and Ferguson, 1991; Newton, 1989). What is required is a description of behaviours, not an evaluation of whether particular responses were effective in helping the individual to cope. (Behavioural outcomes and evaluation of coping effectiveness may be obtained as part of the third phase of CIA.)

It may also be informative to learn whether other people responded to the stress which the focal person was experiencing. For instance, the focal person might indicate that a colleague gave him some advice on how to get the report completed quickly, hence providing social and/or practical support. In some situations, the actions of other people may be as influential or even more influential on outcomes than those taken by the focal person, so it is important to obtain information about the coping *resources* available to and utilized by individuals in stressful transactions.

In sum, the key element in this phase of the CIA procedure is specific description of actual responses displayed when confronted with the situation, rather than global statements about how the person felt. These responses may have involved direct action taken by the individual (1) to deal with the situation him/herself or (2) to seek assistance from others. On the other hand, the person may have taken very little or no direct action, but reframed his/her cognitions or emotional reactions to the incident. Both overt and 'internal' responses are recorded for later analysis and categorization.

Behavioural consequences

The final step in critical incident analysis involves obtaining from individuals a description of the outcomes or consequences of their behaviours during the stressful transaction. Two sets of questions may be utilized during this phase, the first focusing solely on *description* (e.g. '*What happened as a result of what you did?*'), the second on *evaluation* of the outcomes to gauge the effectiveness of a person's coping behaviours (e.g. '*How did you feel about what happened?*'). For instance, an individual might report that talking with the boss led to a clearer understanding of each other's perspective and clarified some problems the subordinate was experiencing in completing the report. Follow-up questions would explore the person's evaluation of these outcomes (e.g. '*I feel very good about this, as this was the first time I'd felt able to explain the difficult conditions I was working under, and she understood my position*').

The focal person in this example favourably evaluated the outcome of his behaviour. In other circumstances, of course, the person's responses to the transaction may produce less favourable consequences. Separation of behavioural efficacy from outcome evaluation avoids confounding of two distinct though related concepts, as well as the imposition of the investigator's value judgements concerning the desirability of outcomes. Descriptive questions focus on the nature of particular behavioural consequences, while evaluative questions explore the person's own assessment of whether those consequences were positive or negative.

INTEGRATION OF STRESSORS, RESPONSES AND OUTCOMES

Once information on specific stressors, behaviours and consequences has been acquired, content analysis is used to code the data into meaningful categories. Following usual prescriptions for content analysis (Krippendorf, 1980; Van Maanen, 1983), independent coders derive category labels and assign individuals' responses to these categories, for each of the three components of the data. Using procedures to analyse frequency data, the resulting coping strategies can then be mapped on to categories of stressor to establish the link between kinds of stressful transaction and the coping behaviours employed by individuals. To complete the chain, further analyses may be conducted to examine the relationship between coping responses and particular outcomes.

PRACTICAL CONSIDERATIONS IN USING CRITICAL INCIDENT ANALYSIS

Critical incident analysis offers several advantages in the study of stress-coping strategies, the most obvious being the ecological validity of information about individuals' responses in specific situations. Direct elicitation of transactions which individuals have actually experienced and consider important to their well-being guarantees that the stressors being investigated are indeed salient to respondents. As noted earlier, other techniques cannot always ensure that the stressors and behaviours being assessed have any real bearing on respondents' functioning.

Secondly, CIA ensures a more accurate portrayal of the specific behaviours which individuals display in response to stressful events. Many existing coping instruments constrain the range of coping responses being assessed (Stone *et al.*, 1991) and contain no mechanism for checking whether the strategies focused upon are those which individuals actually use (Cox and Ferguson, 1991). The information generated from critical incident analysis of coping provides a more comprehensive framework for examining the relationship between behaviours and the environments in which they occur.

Finally, this approach enables a closer examination of the outcomes of situationally-specific coping behaviours. Rather than asking global questions about coping effectiveness, CIA probes the specific consequences for individuals of their responses, along with their evaluation of the outcomes of those responses. Differentiation between description and evaluation of outcomes avoids the confounding of these variables which frequently has occurred in coping research to date (Cohen, 1987), hence enriching our understanding of the consequences of coping strategies and their meaning for individuals experiencing stress.

There are, nevertheless, some potential difficulties which need to be addressed when using a critical incident approach to coping assessment. One of the most problematical concerns level of specificity. This can emerge in two ways. First, respondents may find it difficult to recall the specific details of a particular transaction, especially if the incident was traumatic for them. Although they may have a vivid memory of the source of stress, they may not be able to accurately report their responses to that situation. With the passing of time, individuals may reframe their behaviour (either positively or negatively), leading to distortions in their descriptions of what they actually did.

While there can be no certain mechanism for protecting against this kind of recall distortion, in contrast to other coping instruments CIA forces respondents to report specific actions and it does not create either a positivity or a negativity bias in recall. CIA interviewers may need to prompt respondents if they are experiencing memory difficulties, but prompting takes the form of rephrasing questions rather than suggesting alternatives. If the person is unable to recall in sufficiently specific detail the events, responses and outcomes which surrounded a particular transaction, this incident would not be included for measurement purposes.

A second form of specificity problem arises in the content analysis of data, when the researcher must decide how broad or specific the categories of stressful incidents and coping response are to be. As with any analysis of qualitative data, consistency in coding is essential, since differences between coders in their approach to content analysis can seriously affect the reliability and validity of critical incident data. In addition, if the derived categories are too broad, information about the interrelationship between stressors and responses may be lost. On the other hand, categories which are too specific may not be generalizable beyond the particular setting in which the data were gathered (Krippendorf, 1980). Finding the appropriate level of specificity is an important aspect in research using this methodology.

Finally, just as coders need to be trained in the process of content analysis, interviewers also need training in the critical incident technique. As with behavioural description interviewing for personnel selection, identifying critical incidents and responses requires a clear understanding of the information being sought and a facility with this kind of interviewing. While time-consuming, thorough preparation of both interviewers and coders is essential for the effective utilization of this approach.

SUMMARY AND CONCLUSION

In this chapter we have overviewed some of the major methodological difficulties encountered in research on coping with stress, noted limitations in extant procedures for identifying coping strategies, and proposed an alternative framework for the assessment of coping with work-related stressors. The critical incident methodology advocated here is not new, and indeed has already been utilized to examine some aspects of stressful transactions, especially identification of stressors. However, the present proposal goes beyond previous suggestions (e.g. Cox and Ferguson, 1991) and empirical endeavours (e.g. Newton and Keenan, 1985), by integrating the analysis of stressful incidents, the responses of individuals to those incidents, and the consequences of coping behaviours which are used in stressful transactions. We believe that this approach offers a methodology for linking coping behaviours to sources of stress in work settings, hence providing more comprehensive information about the stress-coping process.

REFERENCES

Aldwin, C. and Revenson, T. (1987) Does coping help? A reexamination of the relation between coping and mental health. *Journal of Personality and Social Psychology*, **53**, 337–48.

Amirkhan, J. (1990) A factor analytically derived measure of coping: The Coping Strategy Indicator. *Journal of Personality and Social Psychology*, **59**, 1066–74.

Billings, A. and Moos, R. (1981) The role of coping responses and social resources in attenuating the stress of life events. *Journal of Behavioral Medicine*, **4**, 139–57.

Billings, A. and Moos, R. (1984) Coping, stress and social resources among adults with unipolar depression. *Journal of Personality and Social Psychology*, **46**, 877–91.

Carver, C., Scheier, M. and Weintraub, J. (1989). Assessing coping strategies: A theoretically based approach. *Journal of Personality and Social Psychology*, **56**, 267–83.

Cohen, F. (1987) Measurement of coping. In S. Kasl and C. Cooper (eds), *Stress and Health: Issues in Research Methodology*, pp. 283–305. Chichester: Wiley.

Cooper, C. (1996) *Handbook of Stress, Medicine and Health*. Boca Raton, Florida: CRC Press.

Cooper, C. and Payne, R. (1988) *Causes, Coping and Consequences of Stress at Work*. Chichester: Wiley.

Cox, T. and Ferguson, E. (1991). Individual differences, stress and coping. In C. Cooper and R. Payne (eds), *Personality and Stress: Individual Differences in the Stress Process*, pp. 7–30. Chichester: Wiley.

Dewe, P. (1991) Primary appraisal, secondary appraisal and coping: Their role in stressful work encounters. *Journal of Occupational Psychology*, **64**, 331–51.

Dewe, P. and Guest, D. (1990) Methods of coping with stress at work: A conceptual analysis and empirical study of measurement issues. *Journal of Organizational Behavior*, **11**, 135–50.

Dewe, P., Cox, T. and Ferguson, E. (1993) Individual strategies for coping with stress at work: A review. *Work and Stress*, **7**, 5–15.

Edwards, J. (1988) The determinants and consequences of coping with stress. In C. Cooper and R. Payne (eds), *Causes, Coping and Consequences of Stress at Work*, pp. 233–63. Chichester: Wiley.

Edwards, J. and Baglioni, A. (1993) The measurement of coping with stress: Construct validity of the Ways of Coping Checklist and the Cybernetic Coping Scale. *Work and Stress*, **7**, 17–31.

Firth-Cozens, J. and Morrison, L. (1986) What stresses health professionals. *British Journal of Clinical Psychology*, **25**, 309–10.

Firth-Cozens, J. and Morrison, L. (1989) Sources of stress and ways of coping in junior house officers. *Stress Medicine*, **5**, 121–6.

Flanagan, J. (1954) The critical incident technique. *Psychological Bulletin*, **51**, 327–58.

Folkman, S. and Lazarus, R. (1980) An analysis of coping in a middle-aged community sample. *Journal of Health and Social Behavior*, **21**, 219–39.

Folkman, S. and Lazarus, R. (1986). If it changes, it must be a process: Study of emotion and coping during three stages of a college examination. *Journal of Personality and Social Psychology*, **48**, 150–70.

Folkman, S., Lazarus, R., Dunkel-Schetter, C., Delongis, A. and Gruen, R. (1986) Dynamics of a stressful encounter: Cognitive appraisal, coping and encounter outcomes. *Journal of Personality and Social Psychology*, **50**, 992–1003.

Holahan, C. and Moos, R. (1990) Life stressors, resistance factors and improved psychological functioning: An extension of the stress resistance paradigm. *Journal of Personality and Social Psychology*, **58**, 909–17.

Kinicki, A. and Latack, J. (1990) Explication of the construct of coping with involuntary job loss. *Journal of Vocational Behavior*, **36**, 339–60.

Krippendorf, K. (1980) *Content Analysis*. London: Sage.

Latack, J. (1986) Coping with job stress: Measures and future directions for scale development. *Journal of Applied Psychology*, **71**, 377–85.

Latack, J. and Havlovic, S. (1992) Coping with job stress: A conceptual evaluation framework for coping measures. *Journal of Organizational Behavior*, **13**, 479–508.

Lazarus, R. and Folkman, S. (1984) *Stress, Appraisal and Coping*. New York: Springer.

Leiter, M. (1991). Coping patterns as predictors of burnout: The function of control and escapist coping patterns. *Journal of Organizational Behavior*, **12**, 123–44.

McCrae, R. (1984) Situational determinants of coping responses: Loss, threat and challenge. *Journal of Personality and Social Psychology*, **46**, 919–28.

Nelson, D. and Sutton, C. (1990) Chronic work stress and coping: A longitudinal study and suggested new directions. *Academy of Management Journal*, **33**, 859–69.

Newton, T. (1989) Occupational stress and coping with stress: A critique. *Human Relations*, **42**, 441–61.

Newton, T. and Keenan, A. (1985) Coping with work-related stress. *Human Relations*, **38**, 107–26.

Parasuraman, S. and Cleek, M. (1984) Coping behaviors and managers' affective reactions to role stressors. *Journal of Vocational Behavior*, **24**, 179–93.

Pearlin, L. and Schooler, C. (1978) The structure of coping. *Journal of Health and Social Behavior*, **19**, 2–21.

Quick, J., Murphy, L. and Hurrell, J. (eds) (1992) Stress and well-being at work: Assessments and interventions for occupational mental health. Washington, DC: American Psychological Association.

Schonfeld, I. (1990) Coping with job-related stress: The case of teachers. *Journal of Occupational Psychology*, **63**, 141–9.

Schwartz, J. and Stone, A. (1993) Coping with daily work problems: Contributions of problem content, appraisals and person factors. *Work and Stress*, **7**, 47–62.

Stone, A. and Neale, J. (1984) New measure of daily coping: Development and preliminary results. *Journal of Personality and Social Psychology*, **46**, 892–906.

Stone, A., Greenberg, M., Kennedy-Moore, E. and Newman, M. (1991) Self-report, situation-specific coping questionnaires: What are they measuring? *Journal of Personality and Social Psychology*, **61**, 648–58.

Van Maanen, J. (1983) *Qualitative Methodology* London: Sage.

West, M. and Savage, Y. (1988a) Coping with stress in health visiting. *Health Visitor*, **61**, 366–8.

West, M. and Savage, Y. (1988b) Visitation of distress. *Nursing Times*, **84**, 43–4.

CHAPTER 11

Stress Management at Work: With Whom, For Whom and To What Ends?

Shirley Reynolds and Rob B. Briner

A critical overview is presented of workplace stress management interventions. It is suggested that they have so far failed to deliver what they have promised. Evaluation studies fail to distinguish between the aims and objectives of primary prevention interventions, such as stress management training, where potential benefits can only be assessed in terms of long-term outcomes, and secondary and tertiary interventions, such as counselling, where existing disorders are treated. Stress management interventions are based on inadequate and oversimplistic theories which obscure the many conflicting interests of employees, employers and researchers, and ignore empirical evidence which suggests that individual well-being, attitudes to work, and work behaviours are minimally linked. It is suggested that alleviating the problems that people experience at work will remain elusive unless the conceptual problems in occupational stress are more fully acknowledged.

INTRODUCTION

The notion that occupational stress is harmful and must be reduced has become received wisdom. It has been suggested elsewhere (Briner and Reynolds, 1993) that occupational stress reduction may, in time, appear to be one of many fads that are initiated by academics, commercialized by consultants and embraced by managers but that ultimately fail to deliver the panacea-like solutions which they promise. There are some signs that a more sceptical attitude towards occupational stress research and the efficacy of occupational stress reduction interventions is emerging. Kahn and Byosiere (1992) and Burke (1993) highlight the puzzling and ever-increasing gap between vigorous practitioner activity in the domain of stress management and the limited evidence that such interventions are effective.

Occupational stress is a compelling and powerful notion. This power is embedded in the belief that occupational stress is a causal factor in the development and maintenance of ill-health. Although the notion of the stress concept has been repeatedly criticized (e.g. Pollock, 1988; Newton, 1989) and the evidence to support the relationship between stress and ill-health is conflicting and inconclusive (O'Leary,

1990; Cohen and Williamson, 1991; Weisse, 1992), even the mere suspicion that stress may cause ill-health has apparently been sufficient to raise concerns about individual well-being and its social, financial and commercial implications.

A stress management industry has developed which attempts to alleviate the supposed effects of occupational stress. Likewise, research on occupational stress is flourishing and supported by government and commercial organizations. One aspect of this research endeavour has been the development of interventions which aim to reduce occupational stress and, it is claimed, promote the well-being and effectiveness of employees. Our intention in this chapter is to evaluate critically the fruits of this research field. The chapter addresses three related questions:

- With whom have stress management interventions been evaluated and to what extent can we expect these participants to benefit?
- For whose benefit are stress management interventions introduced?
- What are the reported effects of these intervention techniques?

STRESS MANAGEMENT – WITH WHOM?

One consideration which has received little attention in the literature on stress management is that of identifying those groups of employees who are the subjects of intervention techniques. As we shall demonstrate in this section, characteristics of employees and of their work environments may be a critical factor in designing suitable intervention strategies, and choosing appropriate designs for outcome studies, and may also constrain the extent to which interventions can be effective.

Conventionally, worksite stress management interventions have been considered to fall into two categories (Newman and Beehr, 1979; Murphy, 1988): those which attempt to develop individuals' skills, techniques and strategies and equip them to deal more effectively with difficult work conditions and demands; and those which attempt to change features of the work environment that are believed to be noxious or harmful to employees. Of these two approaches, individually oriented interventions have been more systematically evaluated (Murphy, 1988; Ivancevich *et al.*, 1990) and are therefore the main focus of this chapter. Interventions which attempt to change organizational or job characteristics are uncommon, commercially unattractive and very often reported in the context of organizational or socio-technical changes rather than as planned interventions with a specific focus on stress reduction (e.g. Wall and Clegg, 1981).

Stress management training (SMT), which tends to be offered to groups of employees, is typically based on multimodal cognitive behaviour therapy (CBT) principles and techniques. Participants are usually taught some form of relaxation or arousal reduction exercise in combination with cognitive techniques based on stress inoculation training, reappraisal or reattribution (Beck, 1976; Meichenbaum, 1985). Training may also include elements of management skills such as time management or interpersonal skills such as delegation and assertiveness. Impacts of SMT appear to be similar to those reported by CBT clients (Reynolds *et al.*, 1993). CBT techniques have been extensively evaluated in the context of treatments for clinical disorders such as anxiety and depression (e.g. Butler *et al.*, 1991; Hollon *et al.*,

1991). Findings from these studies demonstrate the efficacy of CBT techniques in clinical settings. However, there is less evidence that they are effective in bringing about change in individuals in non-clinical settings who may not actually be distressed.

There are a number of key differences between the clinical application of CBT and the worksite application of these techniques in SMT. These differences limit the extent to which we can generalize from the outcomes of CBT in clinical settings to outcomes of SMT using CBT principles. The first is the limited extent to which SMT is designed to meet the specific needs of participants. Individual clients in therapy receive treatment which is based on a thorough assessment of their specific difficulties. Throughout the course of therapy, client and therapist reassess the impact of treatment and adjust therapeutic goals and strategies as necessary. Ivancevich and Matteson (1987) have recommended that all worksite stress reduction interventions should be designed on the basis of a thorough needs assessment. This would include assessing relevant job and organizational characteristics, levels of organizational and social support at work, existing and potential coping strategies, and levels of distress amongst the population. There is little evidence from the literature that this recommendation has been adopted in practice: SMT is typically offered in a packaged, pre-programmed format (Kahn and Byosiere, 1992).

This packaged approach to SMT gives rise to two different problems. The first is that potentially heterogeneous groups of employees with distinctive work demands, home demands, and levels of distress are offered the same training package which may suit their needs to varying degrees. The second problem concerns the extent to which problems experienced by groups of participants in SMT are amenable to individually-oriented interventions. For example, there may be organizational processes which constrain the individual's ability to deal with problems (Menzies, 1960; Handy, 1988), such as implicit negative assumptions about those who admit to personal difficulties, or inadequate support for new procedures such as delegation or time management (Reynolds and Shapiro, 1991). Additionally, the face validity of individually-oriented interventions for prospective participants is compromised if employees perceive problems to be primarily caused by organizational features such as structural or managerial problems, insufficient resources and high workloads.

A second distinction between CBT and SMT is the level of distress reported by clients and participants. SMT participants are usually recruited on a voluntary basis from the working population. Most evaluation studies report levels of psychological well-being amongst participants in the normal, i.e. non-clinical, range. For example, Sallis et al. (1987) used the Beck Depression Inventory (BDI) (Beck et al., 1961) to assess levels of depression before and after SMT. Average pre-intervention BDI scores were 7.2, exactly the same as general population norms for the BDI reported by Nietzel et al. (1987). Clients in psychotherapy outcome studies typically begin treatment with mean BDI scores of 27 (Nietzel et al., 1987) which fall to 12 after treatment and are maintained at follow-up. Within clinical outcome trials a critical distinction is made between clinically and statistically significant change (Jacobson et al., 1984). Statistically significant change is largely dependent on sample size and the power of the statistical test used; clinically significant change is the extent to which the intervention brings about change that is sufficiently substantial to improve client functioning. The extent to which clinically significant change (i.e.

change that will be of sustained benefit to participants) can be expected in the context of SMT is very limited.

Average scores in an unselected group of SMT participants may, of course, obscure the possibility that a minority of participants will experience clinical or sub-clinical levels of distress. There appears to have been little attention given to the possible impact of SMT (including any potential harmful effects) on this sub-group. In principle it seems unlikely that a brief, packaged SMT programme will be beneficial to distressed employees. Moveover, it is unclear if the professional backgrounds and experience of many trainers running SMT are sufficient either to enable them to recognize those participants for whom SMT may be unsuitable, or to contain levels of emotional distress which may be evoked by SMT.

A third difference between SMT and individual CBT concerns the general aims of these interventions. As one might expect given an intervention where the participants are taken from a non-clinical population, Murphy (1988) suggests that most SMT programmes are preventive in orientation. Prevention can be classified as primary, secondary or tertiary (Price *et al.*, 1980). The aim of SMT appears to be primary prevention in that it aims to reduce the incidence of a disorder within a population and typically is directed at individuals who are 'normal' but 'at risk'. The efficacy of primary prevention can therefore be best evaluated by using large samples and assessing the incidence of disorder in the medium to long term. SMT outcome studies report follow-ups of between three months and six months, and sample sizes of less than 80 participants for whom the probability of future disorder is unknown. These design shortcomings make it impossible to assess the efficacy of SMT as a primary prevention strategy.

In short, then, there are major and significant differences between individual CBT and SMT programmes which make it invalid to expect that the outcomes of CBT will be observed when similar principles are applied in a group stress management intervention. Conventionally, group SMT and individual counselling services for occupational stress have been considered under the general category of individually-oriented stress management interventions. However, we would argue strongly that this classification, based on the fact that the individual employee is the unit of change, obscures the crucial difference between the two approaches. SMT provides healthy, non-distressed employees with a range of strategies and techniques which they can use to manage work demands. Worksite counselling and psychotherapy services aim to treat distressed individuals with a disorder or problem that may be irrelevant or peripheral to their work.

Individual therapy and counselling can be considered as either secondary prevention (early and prompt intervention to reduce the duration of a disorder) or tertiary prevention (intervention to reduce the disabling properties of a disorder). Intervention can be expected to bring about relatively rapid and substantial change. Follow-up assessments indicate that the majority of clients report that these gains are maintained for one to two years after treatment. The application of psychotherapy and counselling to deal with work-related difficulties is increasing. Counselling services may be offered in the context of Employee Assistance Programmes (EAPs) which provide a range of welfare, information and support (Murphy, 1988; Berridge and Cooper, 1993). Other organizations have introduced specialized counselling services for staff. In 1986 the UK Post Office employed two counsellors within the

Occupational Healt⟨h Department⟩ ⟨Allison⟩ *et al.* (1989) found that the service was used by employees ⟨from all parts of the⟩ ⟨or⟩ganization (see Chapter 7). In a cursory classification of pr⟨esenting problems,⟩ m⟨a⟩ny appeared to be bringing difficulties which were only pe⟨ripherally related to the⟩ir jobs (e.g. mental health problems such as depression and ⟨anxiety, or marital diffic⟩ulties) and which might usually be dealt with by generic me⟨ntal health services.⟩

An additional feature of SMT and counselling evaluation studies is that they have mostly been offered to professional or clerical employees, often in public sector organizations. Private sector organizations and manual workers have been underrepresented in the literature (an exception to this is reported by Murphy and Sorenson, 1988). The reason for this bias is unclear: it is possible that SMT is offered to white-collar employees on the assumption that they have more discretion at work to apply behavioural and cognitive techniques. Whatever the reason, the extent to which results from this selected working population can be generalized to other working groups is uncertain.

In summary, then, SMT and counselling services are distinctive interventions with different aims, different participants, and different possible outcomes, each of which should influence the design of evaluation research. Typical SMT participants are a heterogeneous group of unselected, non-distressed, white-collar employees for whom the potential benefits of SMT can only be assessed in terms of prevention from later disorder. SMT aims to provide these participants with a range of diverse skills and techniques which they can use to help deal with work demands. Employees using worksite counselling or work-related psychotherapy constitute a more homogeneous group of distressed employees for whom the principal aim of counselling or psychotherapy is to alleviate these psychological difficulties and where improvement can be expected in the short term.

STRESS MANAGEMENT – FOR WHOM? *Who will benefit from Stress Management*

One of the attractive features of stress management interventions is the assumption that benefits will be substantial and widespread. Models of stress suggest that occupational stress is a causal factor in a diverse range of individual and organizational ills. For example, Ivancevich and Matteson (1980) suggest that the personal consequences of occupational stress include coronary heart disease, rheumatic arthritis, ulcers, allergies, headaches, depression and anxiety. Cooper and Marshall (1976) list manifestations of stress as diverse as individual health behaviours such as smoking, poor mental health (e.g. low motivation and low self-esteem) and a range of chronic and acute physical problems including ulcers, high cholesterol levels and heart disease. A similarly diverse range of organizational problems is also proposed which includes absenteeism, low productivity and turnover. The implication of such models is that if means can be found to reduce levels of occupational stress, then beneficial effects will be observed in each of these individual and organizational outcomes. The promise of occupational stress interventions is uniquely attractive in offering substantial and meaningful benefits to employees and employers (and also to the profitability of the organization).

It is both surprising and unsatisfactory that the extraordinary optimism, psychological naivety and selective attention to empirical research which sustains these beliefs has gone almost unchallenged. Even casual reflection makes it clear that diverse organizational problems and diverse individual problems are complex, multifaceted and have multiple causes. How then is it possible that a single, relatively simple intervention could have the universal positive effects which are expected? An additional problem associated with this simplistic view of organizations is that a model which proposes that a single intervention will offer common and equal value to all stakeholders ignores any consideration of conflicts between personal, group and organizational goals. For example, in individually-oriented interventions, participants may be encouraged to articulate and evaluate their own personal goals and needs. Some interventions may challenge assumptions that occupational commitment is essential to individual well-being or that self-worth is dependent on success at work. Thus, in counselling, a legitimate and positive outcome for an individual employee might be to seek alternative employment which better suits their personal needs. In this respect, for example, one organizational outcome of counselling could be an *increase* in turnover amongst employees.

On an empirical basis there is little convincing evidence that employees' well-being or job perceptions are substantively related to organizational outcomes (Guest, 1992). For example, a common assertion is that absenteeism from work is related to psychological and physical well-being which is, in turn, related to occupational stress. There are, however, few empirical studies which examine this chain of relationships and those that exist are conflicting. Jamal (1984) reported correlations of $r = 0.23$ to $r = 0.37$ between stressors and subsequent absence frequency (i.e. job stress accounted for approximately 5–14% of the variance in absence). Less impressively, Gupta and Beehr (1979) reported correlations in the range of $r = 0.13$ to $r = 0.16$ between job stress and absenteeism (1.5–2.5% of the variance in absenteeism), and Spector and Jex (1991) found no significant relationships between absence and job satisfaction or any job characteristics as rated by employees or by independent raters. Johns (1991) has argued that empirical studies which attempt to account for the variance in work behaviours such as absence or turnover from attitudinal or psychological variables are inevitably disappointing because these work behaviours are substantially constrained in their variance by organizational, social and individual factors. The corollary of this argument is that interventions which attempt to influence work behaviours by psychological means alone may also be similarly disappointing.

There appears, then, to be little in the way of a rational basis to support expectations of global benefits of occupational stress interventions, and little empirical basis for the supposed links between individual well-being and organizational outcomes. Yet research and practice adopting these assumptions continue to be widely supported. We propose three reasons for the continued interest in occupational stress research. The first of these is motivated by humanitarian concern for the well-being of individual workers. Within this perspective, research on occupational stress extends to occupational health and welfare services where the specific focus of interests is the well-being of the worker and a subsidiary (but not insignificant) focus is organizational efficiency and profit. A second reason is motivated by a simple belief that reducing occupational stress will result in increased productivity and profitability.

A third, less explicit reason for the recent managerial enthusiasm for stress management interventions may be motivated by fear of employee litigation. Matteson and Ivancevich (1987) and others have reported the increased incidence in the USA of employees successfully suing their employers for psychological or physical damage attributed to stressful working conditions. On the basis that what is observed in the USA is often imported into the UK, some researchers have predicted that UK employers will increasingly provide occupational health and occupational stress services for their employees as a defensive strategy aimed at avoiding subsequent litigation.

Evidence to support this third explanation may be found in the repeated observation that stress management research and practice is overwhelmingly dominated by *evidence of this* interventions which focus on changing individual employees rather than interventions designed to improve features of the working environment (Kahn and Byosiere, 1992; Burke, 1993). The initial enthusiasm with which occupational psychologists (and trade unionists) welcomed such opportunities has yet to be reflected in published empirical research. Neale *et al.* (1982) report that trade union members and officials are more likely to endorse interventions which seek to reduce or eliminate noxious job demands and involve technical, organizational, strategic or policy changes. In contrast, managers and employers are supportive of intervention strategies which focus on the employee as the vehicle for change, which offer personal strategies for dealing with work demands, and which do not involve any meaningful or disruptive organizational-level response.

Often overlooked is the part which external consultants and researchers play in influencing the development and maintenance of the stress management industry. Although the professional identities and roles of these external agents differ, in many ways they are similar in that both have interests in sustaining managerial enthusiasm for the application of stress management interventions. Researchers and consultants advocate the importance of manipulating organizational and job characteristics in order to reduce work demands. However, their ability to initiate and manage organizational-level intervention projects is compromised by conflicting values. Consultants operate in a commercial environment in which income generation is of prime importance. Researchers operate in an academic climate that is increasingly preoccupied by publication rates and income from research grants. Successful research and consultancy in the area of stress management interventions therefore depends primarily on the active co-operation of managers and will inevitably reflect the bias and orientation of this group. The biggest compromise is perhaps necessary for those who combine the roles of consultant and researcher, although even for researchers who have no need of external funding, access to organizational groups is dependent on the relationship between the researcher and representatives of the organization. Research efforts are therefore most likely to reflect the immediate practical needs of organizations and to neglect the development of theory or methodology.

In addition to these problems, Shipley and Orlans (1988) have suggested that the traditional quantitative and scientific orientation of these external agents results in them adopting an 'expert' role that has unforeseen consequences for research and practice in stress management intervention. They argue that the 'expert' role inevitably imposes a distance between researchers or consultants and their 'subjects', which is reinforced by the dominant notions of scientific objectivity. This has practical implications because the concept of 'subject' is one that inhibits action, self-awareness and change. Thus most stress intervention research undermines the very change and action which it hopes to mobilize.

Stress management interventions are presented as universally beneficial and relatively cost-free. We have suggested that such notions of universal benefit can only be sustained by ignoring theoretical and empirical complexities. There are some studies which have assessed the impact of stress management interventions to individual employees and to organizations, and it is these studies which are the focus of the following section.

STRESS MANAGEMENT – TO WHAT ENDS?

The need to evaluate strategies for managing job stress was identified by Newman and Beehr (1979) who concluded that although many strategies had been described, few, if any, had been systematically evaluated. More recently, Ivancevich *et al.* (1990) stated that 'present knowledge about SMIs [stress management interventions] is largely based on anecdotes, testimonials, and methodologically weak research' (p. 259). This negative conclusion is partly echoed by other reviewers, most of whom identify methodological weaknesses in the majority of studies (e.g. DeFrank and Cooper, 1987; Murphy, 1984; 1988) but who typically suggest that there are grounds for qualified optimism about the potential benefits of SMT to individual employees. The aim of this section is to examine the extent to which individuals and organizations can be said to benefit from stress management interventions.

Benefits to the individual employee

Stress management interventions are generally claimed to provide psychological and physical benefits to participants. A number of studies have evaluated SMT in controlled trials. Sallis *et al.* (1987) allocated 76 participants to one of three conditions: multicomponent SMT; relaxation training; and an education support group. Psychological well-being, job satisfaction, work stress, resting blood pressure and blood pressure reactivity were assessed prior to any intervention, at the end of the eight-week intervention period, and at three-month follow-up. After all three interventions there were significant reductions in anxiety, depression and hostility which were maintained at follow-up, but there were no significant reductions in job satisfaction, work stress or either of the blood pressure measures.

The authors identified two important issues. The first was the fact that participants in all three conditions made similar gains, which suggests that any benefits were due to non-specific factors of the interventions such as group support and encouragement rather than to the supposed 'active' components of stress management training and relaxation. In other words, perhaps any group intervention which enabled participants to discuss issues of importance in a supportive atmosphere could have had the same effects. The second issue concerns the extent of changes observed in this non-clinical sample. As we have discussed above, bringing about meaningful change in individual well-being when participants are not initially distressed is somewhat difficult. At baseline assessment, participants' blood pressure and psychological well-being were within normal limits. Not surprisingly, no changes were observed in blood pressure. Although there were statistically significant changes in some of the self-report variables, these were of a modest size and unlikely to be of clinical significance to the participants themselves.

Another well-controlled study by Ganster et al. (1982) allocated participants to an immediate treatment condition and a delayed waiting control group. Ganster et al. found that in the immediate condition there were statistically significant changes in psychological well-being; however, these were modest and were not replicated in the delayed control group. The authors concluded that there were inadequate grounds for recommending the widespread adoption of SMT.

Bruning and Frew (1987) compared the impact of 8–10 hours of training in exercise, relaxation and management skills on physiological measures of pulse rate, diastolic and systolic blood pressure and galvanic skin response. After training, each of the three conditions resulted in broadly equivalent and significant reductions in pulse rate and systolic blood pressure. A control group of volunteers who received education and information about stress did not show similar gains. The obvious strengths of this study are the random allocation of participants to active and control treatments and the nature of the outcome variables which are unlikely to be subject to attributional or self-report bias. As the authors themselves comment, these physiological changes do not of themselves indicate improved physical health; moreover, the study did not examine the extent to which these changes were maintained after training was completed.

As we have stated above, we see a major distinction between group SMT and individual counselling or psychotherapy for distressed workers. Advocates of EAPs often claim uniformly positive results. Indicators of EAP success include the percentage of employees using the service, the percentage returning to work after treatment, and the cost savings to the company. Murphy (1988) comments that, using these criteria, EAPs appear to be very successful, with 50 per cent of workers returning to work, and apparently large cost savings based on reduced absenteeism and health care costs. However, these findings are based on methodologically flawed evidence. Control groups and random allocation to treatment are not common and there is evidence of considerable selection bias into EAPs (Swanson and Murphy, 1991). There is, though, considerable evidence from the psychotherapy research literature which suggests that psychotherapy and counselling for work-related difficulties may be effective. Meta-analytic reviews (e.g. Smith et al., 1980; Shapiro and Shapiro, 1982) conclude that the benefits of psychotherapy compared to no-treatment have been established and that all modes of therapy appear to have broadly equivalent outcomes.

Two recent studies have demonstrated that counselling and psychotherapy is of substantial benefit to distressed workers. Allison et al. (1989) evaluated the effects of a workplace counselling service for Post Office workers. Employees using the service completed measures of psychological well-being before counselling and after counselling. Results indicated that mean levels of depression and anxiety were significantly reduced after counselling. Firth-Cozens and Shapiro (1986) evaluated the effects of psychotherapy on 40 professional and managerial employees whose psychological problems were affecting their work. After therapy, clients reported substantial benefits in terms of decreased depression and anxiety which were sustained at two–year follow-up (Shapiro and Firth–Cozens, 1990).

As we have already suggested, SMT can only be meaningfully evaluated as a primary prevention strategy. Short-term physiological and psychological changes may be maintained after training and may, in principle, provide protection against the development of chronic mental and physical disorder. However, the current state of research does not provide any evidence of such benefits. Counselling and psychotherapy services appear to bring about more substantial benefits to individual employees, but need to be evaluated in their own terms rather than as *stress* reduction interventions.

Benefits to the organization

Very few studies have evaluated the impact of stress management interventions on organizational-level outcomes such as performance, absenteeism or turnover (Ivancevich *et al.*, 1990). Where work-related variables are assessed, SMT outcome studies generally rely on self-reported work attitudes or perceptions such as job satisfaction or perceived job stress (e.g. Sallis *et al.*, 1987) and these appear not to change. Murphy and Sorensen (1988) report the impact of two forms of SMT (relaxation training and biofeedback) on performance ratings, absenteeism, accidents and work injuries in road maintenance workers. Relaxation training was associated with reduced absenteeism in the year following training. None of the other outcome variables were significantly reduced in either of the two treatment groups, and reductions in absence were no longer observed at the third assessment (1½ years after training). The authors concluded that SMT has little or no impact on employee behaviours and was probably best utilized in conjunction with organizational change interventions.

Moving away from group SMT programmes, there may be more reason to expect generalized benefits from counselling and psychotherapy approaches. Psychological problems such as depression and anxiety are often accompanied by impairments of memory, concentration and motivation. For this reason there is good cause to assume that successful treatment of these disorders will result in improved work performance. Mintz *et al.* (1992) reviewed the effects of treatments for depression on work impairment. Ten treatment studies in which work outcomes were evaluated were identified. Functional work impairment such as unemployment, absenteeism and self-reported work problems was common at baseline. Results indicated that work outcomes appeared to improve following treatment but that these improvements lagged behind symptomatic change in depression.

This review provides encouraging evidence for the efficacy of psychotherapy for work-related problems. However, in most of the studies reviewed, work impairment was of marginal interest. A few studies have focused specifically on work-related problems and work outcomes. In the Post Office study (Allison *et al.*, 1989) counselling resulted in significantly reduced absenteeism. There was, however, no evidence that improved attendance was accompanied by improved performance; in fact, job satisfaction decreased and other variables such as organizational commitment did not change after counselling. Firth-Cozens and Hardy (1992) examined work perceptions amongst 90 white-collar, professional and managerial workers who received psychotherapy. As symptom levels were reduced, work perceptions became more positive; perceptions of social support at work, control and skill use were most improved; perceptions of variety and clarity in the job showed little change.

Although there are relatively few studies which have evaluated organizational-level stress management interventions, these are worthy of particular notice here because one might expect these interventions to bring about the most dramatic benefits at an organizational level. A small number of organizational-level studies are repeatedly cited in reviews of stress management interventions (Wall and Clegg, 1981; Jackson, 1983; Pierce and Newstrom, 1983). Although most reviewers have suggested that these provide encouraging evidence for the efficacy of changing organizational characteristics, each provides only partial support. More recently, Jones *et al.* (1988) reported an interesting example of an intervention study and replication which combined individual and organizational-level interventions. In two preliminary studies, the authors established that high levels of perceived stress amongst hospital staff were associated with the incidence of medical malpractice. A complex intervention strategy was developed which consisted of assessing perceived stress levels, communicating these findings to managers and staff, negotiating policy and procedural changes aimed at reducing sources of stress for employees, providing SMT modules to all staff, and implementing an EAP. Twenty-two hospitals received the intervention and 22 other hospitals acted as matched controls. Following the intervention period, malpractice claims in the experimental group fell from 31 in the year before the intervention to 9 per year after the intervention. In the control group of hospitals, malpractice claims in the corresponding time periods were unchanged: 36 claims and 35 claims respectively.

The results of this study are impressive but somewhat difficult to evaluate. Given the complex nature of the intervention, it is impossible to assess which aspects were instrumental in bringing about change. In addition, Jones *et al.* report only one outcome variable in their two intervention studies, and other research demonstrates that change may not be so uniformly positive. For example, Wall *et al.* (1986) used a quasi-experimental design to study the effects of introducing autonomous work groups in a manufacturing company. Autonomous work groups enable employees to exercise more control and self-determination over their day-to-day work. According to the job characteristics model (Hackman and Oldham, 1976), this degree of control is expected to be intrinsically motivating to employees, to increase mental health, and to lead to improved group performance and reduced turnover. As expected, job satisfaction amongst shop-floor workers did increase, but there were no beneficial effects on mental health, work motivation or performance. Unexpectedly, turnover increased after the intervention, and managers reported increased levels of personal stress. Similar mixed findings were reported by Cordery *et al.* (1991) who examined the impact of introducing autonomous work groups in mineral processing plants. Job satisfaction and organizational commitment significantly improved after the intervention, but turnover and absenteeism significantly increased.

Taken together, these two studies suggest that the impact of organizational change is complex and involves positive and negative outcomes. Little evidence supports the claims that SMT brings about organizational benefits, and individual, psychological benefits are small and short-lived. It is therefore extremely unlikely that the uniformly beneficial results which are promised implicitly and explicitly by occupational stress practitioners and researchers will ever occur in practice. Much attention has been focused on the ethical problems involved in providing individual stress management interventions (e.g. Ganster *et al.*, 1982). There are, however, clear ethical problems involved in *all* interventions, and these are, if anything, more complex where the aim of the intervention is to bring about organizational change.

CONCLUSION

Occupational stress in general, and occupational stress interventions in particular, have been the focus of much interest and enthusiasm from academic and non-academic groups. This chapter has attempted to provide a partial explanation for this intense interest and to explore some of the reasons for the failure of occupational stress interventions to deliver what they promise. Our review of the stress management literature reflects our critical view of current research and practice. Other reviewers have presented a more optimistic picture, recommending methodological improvements and increased focus on organizationally-oriented interventions (e.g. Ivancevich *et al.*, 1990; Murphy, 1988).

Our position is that the whole area of occupational stress management research requires urgent and fundamental reconsideration. Most importantly, we need to establish a clearer understanding of *exactly* what it is that stress management training is attempting to manage. Further key tasks include clarifying the likely and desired outcomes of different intervention strategies, acknowledging the complex relationships between individual well-being, organizational performance and work attitudes, and establishing the differing motives which sustain the enthusiasm of employers and workers for stress management interventions.

Even more urgently, we believe that occupational stress researchers and practitioners must become aware of their own conflicting roles and values and the extent to which these hamper the development of useful, applicable and theoretically sound research. There is clearly a commitment to improve the working conditions of employees and to increase the profitability and effectiveness of work organizations. However, these two desirable outcomes may often be incompatible, and stress research and practice has obscured and minimized the inevitable conflict between them. Occupational stress researchers and consultants have fallen into the trap of trying to please all of the people all of the time. Researchers and researched, consultants and clients, each have unrealistic expectations of the potential benefits of stress management interventions. Stress research is in serious danger of being recognized as yet another short-lived fad unless a more reasoned, measured and critical approach is taken by its most vocal proponents. Without a fuller conceptual grasp of the problems people experience at work and the possible consequences of such problems, the means to alleviate them will remain elusive.

REFERENCES

Allison, T., Cooper, C.L. and Reynolds, P. (1989) Stress counselling in the workplace: The Post Office experience. *The Psychologist*, **2**, 384–8.

Beck, A.T. (1976) *Cognitive Therapy and the Emotional Disorders.* New York: International Universities Press.

Beck, A.T., Ward, C., Mendelsohn, M., Mock, J. and Erbaugh, J. (1961) An inventory for measuring depression. *Archives of General Psychiatry*, **4**, 53–63.

Berridge, J. and Cooper, C.L. (1993) Stress and coping in US organizations: The role of the Employee Assistance Programme. *Work and Stress*, **7**, 89–102.

Briner, R.B. and Reynolds, S.A. (1993) Bad theory and bad practice in occupational stress. *The Occupational Psychologist*, **19**, 8–13.

Bruning, N.S. and Frew, D.R. (1987) Effects of exercise, relaxation and management skills training on physiological stress indicators: A field experiment. *Journal of Applied Psychology*, **72**, 515–21.

Burke, R.J. (1993) Interventions to reduce occupational stressors. *Work and Stress*, **7**, 77–88.

Butler, G., Fennell, M., Robson, P. and Gelder, M. (1991) Comparison of behavior therapy and cognitive behavior therapy in the treatment of generalized anxiety disorder. *Journal of Consulting and Clinical Psychology*, **59**, 167–75.

Cohen, S. and Williamson, G.M. (1991) Stress and infectious disease in humans. *Psychological Bulletin*, **109**, 5–24.

Cooper, C.L. and Marshall, J. (1976) Occupational sources of stress: A review of the literature relating to coronary heart disease and mental ill health. *Journal of Occupational Psychology*, **49**, 11–28.

Cordery, J.T., Mueller, W.S. and Smith, L.M. (1991) Attitudinal and behavioral effects of autonomous group working: A longitudinal field study. *Academy of Management Journal*, **34**, 464–76.

DeFrank, R.S. and Cooper, C.L. (1987) Worksite stress management interventions: Their effectiveness and a conceptualization. *Journal of Managerial Psychology*, **2**, 4–10.

Firth, J.A. and Shapiro, D.A. (1986) An evaluation of psychotherapy for job-related distress. *Journal of Occupational Psychology*, **59**, 111–19.

Firth-Cozens, J.A. and Hardy, G.E. (1992) Occupational stress, clinical treatment and changes in job perceptions. *Journal of Occupational and Organizational Psychology*, **65**, 81–8.

Ganster, D.C. and Mayes, B.T., Sime, W.E. and Tharp, G.D. (1982) Managing organizational stress: A field experiment. *Journal of Applied Psychology*, **67**, 533–42.

Guest, D. (1992) The continuing search for the happy, productive worker. Working paper, Birkbeck College, Department of Occupational Psychology.

Gupta, N. and Beehr, T.A. (1979) Job stress and employee behaviors. *Organizational Behavior and Human Performance*, **23**, 373–87.

Hackman, J.R. and Oldham, G.R. (1976) Motivation through the design of work: Test of a theory. *Organizational Behavior and Human Performance*, **15**, 250–79.

Handy, J. (1988) Theoretical and methodological problems within occupational stress and burnout research. *Human Relations*, **41**, 351–69.

Hollon, S.D., Shelton, R.C. and Loosen, P.T. (1991) Cognitive therapy and pharmacotherapy for depression. *Journal of Consulting and Clinical Psychology*, **59**, 88–99.

Ivancevich, J.M. and Matteson, M.T. (1980) *Stress and Work: A Managerial Perspective*. Glenview: Scott Foresman.

Ivancevich, J.M. and Matteson, M.T. (1987) Organizational level stress management interventions: A review and recommendations. *Journal of Organizational Behavioural Management*, **81**, 229–48.

Ivancevich, J.M., Matteson, M.T., Freedman, S.M. and Phillips, J.S. (1990) Worksite stress management interventions. *American Psychologist*, **45**, 252–61.

Jackson, S.E. (1983) Participation in decision making as a strategy for reducing job-related strain. *Journal of Applied Psychology*, **38**, 404–24.

Jacobson, N.S., Follette, W.C. and Ravenstorf, D. (1984) Psychotherapy outcome research; methods for reporting variability and evaluating clinical significance. *Behavior Therapy*, **15**, 336–52.

Jamal, M. (1984) Job stress and job performance controversy: An empirical assessment. *Organizational Behavior and Human Performance*, **33**, 1–21.

Johns, G. (1991) Substantive and methodological constraints on behavior and attitudes in organizational research. *Organizational Behavior and Human Decision Processes*, **49**, 105–23.

Jones, J.W., Barge, B.N., Steffy, B.D., Fay, L.M., Kunz, L.K. and Wuebker, L.J. (1988) Stress and medical malpractice: Organizational risk assessment and intervention. *Journal of Applied Psychology*, **73**, 727–35.

Kahn, R.L. and Byosiere, P. (1992) Stress in organizations. In M.D. Dunnette and L.M. Hough (eds), *Handbook of Industrial and Organizational Psychology*, Vol. III. Palo Alto, CA: Consulting Psychologists Press.

Matteson, M.T. and Ivancevich, J.M. (1987) *Controlling Work Stress: Effective Human Resource and Management Strategies*. London: Jossey-Bass.

Meichenbaum, D. (1985) *Stress Inoculation Training*. New York: Pergamon Press.

Menzies, I. (1960) Nurses under stress. *International Nursing Review*, **7**, 9–16.

Mintz, J., Mintz, L.I., Arruda, M.J. and Hwang, S.S. (1992) Treatment of depression and functional capacity to work. *Archives of General Psychiatry*, **49**, 761–8.

Murphy, L.R. (1984) Occupational stress management: A review and appraisal. *Journal of Occupational Psychology*, **57**, 1–15.

Murphy, L.R. (1988) Workplace interventions for stress reduction and prevention. In C.L. Cooper and R. Payne (eds), *Causes, Coping and Consequences of Stress at Work*. Chichester: Wiley.

Murphy, L.R. and Sorenson, S. (1988) Employee behaviors before and after stress management. *Journal of Occupational Behavior*, **9**, 173–82.

Neale, M.S., Singer, J., Schwartz, G.E. and Schwartz, J. (1982) Conflicting perspectives on stress reduction in occupational settings: A systems approach to their resolution. Report to NIOSH on P.O. No. 82–1058, Cincinnati, OH.

Newman, J.E. and Beehr, T.A. (1979) Personal and organizational strategies for handling job stress: A review of research and opinion. *Personnel Psychology*, **32**, 1–43.

Newton, T.J. (1989) Occupational stress and coping with stress. *Human Relations*, **42**, 441–61.

Nietzel, M.T., Russell, R.L., Hemmings, K.A. and Gretter, M.L. (1987) Clinical significance of psychotherapy for unipolar depression: A meta-analytic approach to social comparison. *Journal of Consulting and Clinical Psychology*, **55**, 156–61.

O'Leary, A. (1990) Stress, emotion and human immune function. *Psychological Bulletin*, **108**, 363–82.

Pierce, J.L. and Newstrom, J.W. (1983) The design of flexible work schedules and employee responses: Relationships and processes. *Journal of Occupational Behavior*, **4**, 247–62.

Pollock, K. (1988) On the nature of social stress: Production of a modern mythology. *Social Science and Medicine*, **26**, 381–92.

Price, R.H., Bader, B.C. and Ketterer, R.F. (1980) Prevention in community mental health. In R.H. Price, R.F. Ketterer, B.C. Bader and J. Monahan (eds), *Prevention in Mental Health*. London: Sage.

Reynolds, S. and Shapiro, D.A. (1991) Stress reduction in transition: Conceptual problems in the design, implementation and evaluation of worksite stress management interventions. *Human Relations*, **44**, 717–33.

Reynolds, S., Taylor, E. and Shapiro, D.A. (1993) Session impact in stress management training. *Journal of Occupational and Organizational Psychology*, **66**, 99–113.

Sallis, J.R., Trevorrow, T.R., Johnson, C.C., Hovell, M.F. and Kaplan, R.M. (1987) Worksite stress management: A comparison of programmes. *Psychology and Health*, **1**, 237–55.

Shapiro, D.A. and Firth-Cozens, J.A. (1990) Two-year follow-up of the Sheffield psychotherapy project. *British Journal of Psychiatry*, **157**, 389–91.

Shapiro, D.A. and Shapiro, D. (1982). Meta-analysis of comparative therapy outcome research: A replication and refinement. *Psychological Bulletin*, **92**, 581–604.

Shipley, P. and Orlans, V. (1988) Stress research: An interactionist perspective. In L.R. Murphy, S.L. Sauter and C.L. Cooper (eds), *Occupational Stress: Issues and Developments in Research.* London: Taylor & Francis.

Smith, M.L., Glass, G.V. and Miller, T.I. (1980) *The Benefits of Psychotherapy.* Baltimore: The John Hopkins University Press.

Spector, P.E. and Jex, S.M. (1991) Relations of job characteristics from multiple data sources with employee affect, absence, turnover intentions and health. *Journal of Applied Psychology*, **76**, 46–53.

Swanson, N.G. and Murphy, L.R. (1991) Mental health counselling in industry. In C.L. Cooper and I.T. Robertson (eds), *International Review of Industrial and Organizational Psychology*, Vol. 6. Chichester: Wiley.

Wall, T.D. and Clegg, C.W. (1981) Individual strain and organizational functioning. *British Journal of Clinical Psychology*, **20**, 135–6.

Wall, T.D., Kemp, N.J., Jackson, P.R. and Clegg, C.W. (1986) Outcomes of autonomous workgroups: A long-term field experiment. *Academy of Management Journal*, **29**, 280–304.

Weisse, C.S. (1992) Depression and immunocompetence: A review of the literature. *Psychological Bulletin*, **111**, 475–89.

Postscript

The previous chapters have provided an overview to the subject of stress and its management both at individual and organizational levels. The different therapeutic approaches highlighted a variety of ways in which individuals may receive stress counselling or stress management. The interventions directed at the prevention of coronary heart disease and at reducing the impact of traumatic stress at work are very encouraging. It was argued that counselling and stress management training were as important as stress audits in meeting the needs of individuals and organizations. The last three chapters raised important issues regarding measurement and other methodological problems. Overall, there was a general agreement that more research in the field of stress management and counselling is needed.

With the increase in litigation against employers for stress at work, we predict more practitioners will enter the lucrative field of stress management. Let us hope that they are appropriately qualified to undertake the work.

Index

Numbers in bold denote chapter/major section devoted to subject